There's No Place Like Nome

By

ARTIS PALMER

ENDICOTT AND HUGH BOOKS

THERE'S NO PLACE LIKE NOME

Copyright © 2013 by Artis Palmer
All rights reserved, including the right to reproduce this book, or portions thereof, in any form. Published by Endicott and Hugh Books, Burton, Washington. www.endicottandhughbooks.com

Publisher's Cataloging-In-Publication Data
(Prepared by The Donohue Group, Inc.)

Palmer, Artis.
   There's no place like Nome / by Artis Palmer. -- Newly rev. ed.

   p. ; cm.

   Originally published: New York : William Morrow & Company, 1963.
   ISBN: 978-0-9837115-9-9 (trade paperback)

   1. Palmer, Artis. 2. Palmer family. 3. Gold mines and mining--Alaska--Nome. 4. Nome (Alaska)--Biography. 5. Nome (Alaska)--Description and travel. I. Title.

F914.N6 P35 2013
979.8/6/00922   2013935685

Book design by Masha Shubin, Editor, Amy Kirkman a.k.a. "Bird bones"
Map by Lily Brim,
Cover Photos: Beautiful Winter Background © Conrado (BigStock-Photo.com), Walrus © Vladsilver (DreamsTime.com), SUMMER SUNRISE © Curaga (DreamsTime.com), Winter Tractor © Moori (DreamsTime.com)

ISBN: 978-0-9837115-9-9 Trade paperback

Printed in the United States of America
10 9 8 7 6 5 4 3 2 1

THERE'S NO PLACE

LIKE NOME

Artis Palmer

To M. and D.,

my technical advisors on Moonshine and Fool's Gold

Nome

Canada

Seattle

S.S. Victoria

AUTHOR'S NOTE

Now, sixty years after this book was written, some things don't change. Again we are in the grip of a long recession, and as the old song has it, "the rich get richer...and the poor get children!"

But ordinary people are still taking extraordinary journeys, just to make a living. As my folks traveled to the back of beyond for the chance of a job in Nome, Alaska in 1930, I now know of a young family who came all the way from Guangzhou, China, to Seattle, Washington, for the promise of a better education for their son, Bao.

I met him at the Beacon Hill Public Library, and after I tutored him for four years through high school, Bao is now studying at the University of Washington on a full scholarship, complete with room and board, books, and high hopes for a major in electrical engineering.

So, once in a while America does something right! We're still mired in another senseless war, the Democrats and Republicans have fought each other into complete gridlock, and global warming looms even closer. However, from all over the world, the people keep coming for a better life, and a lot of them find it.

I am still proud to be a citizen of the United State of America.

Artis Palmer
Seattle, 2013

CHAPTER 1

My mother always says that if there is one year she could pick out of all the rest and throw away completely, that one would be 1930. It was one of those years when, if you dropped your bread and butter, you knew it would land jelly-side down. The rainfall for Seattle broke all records since 1890, and Mama had her thirtieth birthday. All in that one year, Shorty had twelve pups in her first litter, the still blew up, Daddy had no job, and as if that weren't enough, Mama was pregnant.

So after going through all that, it was no wonder when the chance came for Daddy to go to work in Nome, Alaska, we went. "About that time we would have taken a job in Tukwila or Timbuktu, or the moon, if they'd been offering them there!" adds Mama.

Of course 1929 was the start of it. Like everyone else, the Palmers went broke late in '29. "I don't know why they called it the crash," Mama continues. "It wasn't nearly that dramatic. Oh sure, a few of the people we knew at the time lost a lot in the stock market, but mostly the world just seemed to grind to a halt. The radio blatted away about 'bulls' and 'bears,' discounts and margins, and then all of a sudden a bunch of rich men started jumping out of their windows. But Jack and I didn't have any stock, and it seemed the whole world was shaking because some Henny-Penny had mentioned that perhaps the sky was falling. It was less than a month before we knew that it *had* fallen.

"We had just finished the Capitol View Apartments, and we'd borrowed almost $200,000 to do it. I kept the books for the whole deal, and why anyone would loan us that kind of money on sheer speculation, I'll never know; but everyone was doing it then. I'm sure you've seen the pictures, Artis. It was that beautiful white terra-cotta building overlooking Puget Sound. It was the biggest thing we'd built up to that time, and we were both so proud. It was kind of like our monument.

"To this day, I can't bear to look at the place when we drive by. It hurts too much. And of course, your father always has to swear and blame it all on poor old Hoover."

Then Mama usually gets the old leather album out, with all the snapshots glued in carefully on the black paper pages. One of my favorites is an early one of Mama at about twenty, in a black sateen dress, sitting very casually astride a motorcycle. Even then she weighed about 170 pounds and had a very large bust which she considered a hideous cross to bear. Then there are the usual funny wedding shots in the droopy, filmy, sexless styles that were popular in 1921. And of course, the Capitol View is prominently displayed. It was a beautiful building, shining and new, with the little construction shack still out in front.

> JOHN W. PALMER, GENERAL CONTRACTOR
> IN SEATTLE SINCE 1921
> FOR SALE

There's even a picture of Mama and Daddy parked out in front of the place in a large Studebaker touring car. But somehow they don't look like the same comfortable people I've always known. They look sassy and slick. They look like Jack and Alice Palmer, a couple of big-time operators who danced the black bottom, and laughed out loud, and made love, and liked jazz.

But that was the year that they found out that man cannot live on jazz alone. That was the year that new houses went out of style, people didn't need new store buildings anymore; and especially, they didn't need the Capitol View Apartments.

However, Rudy, the brick mason, did need his $10,000; the plumber had to have his $4,950; and they owed the electrician almost $3,000. The only thing to do was borrow, and it seemed that everyone in Seattle had the same idea. Dad waited in the office of the mortgage company for four and a half days before he was able to start making the arrangements to sell his soul. By the time he negotiated a second mortgage on the building, which enabled him to pay off most of the sub-contractors, The Palmer Construction Company had lost every dime they'd been building on for the past ten years. Mama and Daddy never quite got over the whole affair.

Finally they managed to sell the Capitol View at an incredible loss, with approximately seven thousand dollars still owing to sub-contractors and building suppliers. The easiest way, of course, would have been to declare the Palmer Construction Company bankrupt, but they were willing to try everything and anything else first. They sold tools, trucks, and equipment, along with excess furniture and personal treasures; but still debts of about five thousand dollars remained like a blight to life itself. Five thousand dollars seems not such a terrible sum now, but in those days it might just as well have been five million; because for the next few years, there were no jobs. The days, and weeks and months, crawled along with broken backs. People clung to every dime they had as if it might be their last. If a door needed fixing, they fixed it themselves or they let it hang open. If a porch roof needed new shingles, there were plenty of thin old men going from door to door asking for a handout who became excellent roofers for that day. And new houses or stores, or garages or theaters were nonexistent. Maybe next year, or the year after . . .

"Grama had plenty of room, so we moved in with her and rented our own house," explains Mama, "so we always had enough to eat. It was finding enough to do that was hard. Oh, your Grama and I could always find little jobs to do, but you know how Daddy is. He'd start out in the morning with long lists of ridiculous things for me to do, and by noontime he'd have it figured out so that the whole depression was caused directly by my inefficient bookkeeping. Nationwide!"

Of course, everyone knew it was only temporary.

However, there's always a way out; and like most crooks, Mama and Daddy fell into the life of crime as easily and naturally as if it were a downy feather bed.

They'd been renting their large old house to one bootlegger after another, as they were the only ones who had money enough to pay rent, and the secluded location was perfect. But after each tenant left, usually after a police raid, the place would be a wreck. They had fires, explosions, fights, leaks in the apparatus, and their housekeeping probably did as much damage as anything else.

Finally, in spite of the fifty a month they'd been getting in rent for the old house, both Mama and Daddy agreed that neither they nor "the ranch," as the family always called our place, could stand any more bootleggers. The last bunch had stolen all the bathroom fixtures when they left, and Mama vowed she would starve before she rented the place again.

They moved back home, and had been cleaning and patching the plumbing for about a week, when Roger Anderson called. He had lived in the ranch some months before and was by far the best of the lot. He was a nice, clean-looking young man, and Mama always said that he looked more like a choirboy than a bootlegger. Daddy told him that they would definitely not consider renting the place again. He went on with the sad story—ruined plumbing, moldy shower curtain, and all—but Roger still wanted to come out. The folks both liked Roger and would be glad to see him. The house had been made almost livable again, and besides they had nothing but time anyway.

As it turned out, Roger Anderson was doing even better than when they had seen him last. He said that he had an outlet for as much whisky as he could make, but that he was too closely watched to be able to make any himself. In other words, he was looking for a partner. As for the Palmers, they were still five thousand dollars in debt, the building business was nonexistent, and as the crowning touch, Mama found that she was going to have a baby.

When Daddy first heard this bit of news, he took it as a deep personal affront. This was definitely not part of his plans for the next few years. But finally he decided to forgive her and chalk the whole thing up to a fatal flaw in Mama's nature, right along with her poor bookkeeping methods which had caused the depression.

So, when Roger Anderson offered them approximately a hundred dollars a day if they would make moonshine for him, the voice of conscience was very small and the debt was still very large. An hour later he left and Mama and Daddy were in the bootlegging business.

"Don't worry, Alice," said Daddy, "Alcatraz can't be so bad. Why, they probably even have a free maternity ward."

CHAPTER 2

Roger Anderson arranged to bring all the supplies and equipment they would need for the new enterprise, and by the end of the next week the Palmers were in full production and learning fast. They soon found that one of the trademarks of the moonshiner was his Dodge, and Roger had a beauty.

His was a nondescript 1919 model with a huge square trunk on the back. In those days the Dodge was built with extra heavy springs which made it perfect for the transportation of heavy equipment, sugar sacks, and full barrels.

Every few days, Roger and his great machine would rumble down Sumerville Street, through the heavily wooded valley, into the Palmer driveway and finally into the large old barn at the back. The house was the only one on the street, and probably no one ever saw him after he left the main highway, four blocks away.

The initial outlay to set up operations was practically nil, as all Roger had to do was disassemble his still, which he had been running at his own home, and move it to the barn. He and Jack laughed and snorted like a couple of boys while they set up the complicated apparatus. Their voices rang through the clear air of the fine fall day, and Mama said it sounded more as if they were building a sailboat than constructing a sour-mash still.

And a lovely still it was, too; 1929 was the year that more people in the state of Washington were killed by bootleg whisky manufactured in these strange and wonderful homemade contraptions than were killed by automobile accidents. But Roger's still was a real professional job. This old girl had known many men during her violent career, but somewhere along the line a chemist must have kept and loved her well. Her limbs and joints were clean-lined and polished smooth, pure copper throughout. She'd been fed only the finest diet of corn sugar and water and yeast, and fired with the highest- grade oil. It couldn't have been more surprising, to open the creaky doors of the sagging, paint-flaked old barn, hear the soft gossip of the hens Grama kept in the back, accustom your eyes to the dim streaks of sunshine filtering through the chinks in the walls, and then come face to face with that gleaming steel and copper and glass beauty. So Mama christened her Rose, and Rose took over as mistress of the barn and of their lives as well.

Rose was a simple mechanism, but she demanded a great deal of time and attention to produce the desired results. She worked under the simple assumption that if you simmer fermented corn sugar, steam it gently, then cool the steam until it condenses to a liquid, you will end up with quite an effective intoxicant. When questioned on just how the stuff actually tasted, Mama becomes evasive.

Dad designed a compact oil burner to heat the large copper vat of mash. This gave the controlled high heat needed and also gave off very little smoke. If anyone had driven by, it would have been difficult to explain a wood and coal fire roaring night and day to keep twenty chickens warm.

It was a quiet Sunday morning when Roger brought the first load of makings. The Dodge was filled to the bursting point with fifty-pound sacks of coarse brown corn sugar and five-pound cakes of yeast. They were all as giddy as new brides with their first recipe, so Roger insisted on stirring up the first batch immediately. He and Jack divided the corn sugar into six wooden barrels. The barrels each held about three hundred gallons and took up almost half the barn, so Rose was crowded close to the chickens who clucked indignantly at the intrusion. The men mashed in the correct amount of yeast and filled each barrel almost to the top with water. Each barrel had a mysterious device that extended down into the bottom, called the fermentation gauge. Roger and

Jack discussed this mechanism sagely and at length like a couple of consulting surgeons. It seemed that the constant temperature was all-important, so none of the hens hatched her eggs any more diligently than Jack attended his precious vats. He kept the oil burner going smoothly night and day, which maddened the hens. Mama was sure the poor old biddies were going to have a nervous breakdown from being awakened a few times every night as Dad came in to check on the fire and his gauges. In spite of the hens, though, the deed was done—the thing was started, and all they had to do was watch and wait.

And although the very best people were doing it, Mama was scared stiff from the first day the sugar and yeast went into the first vat until the last drop was sold. Even though bootlegging became America's most popular indoor sport, this didn't make it right to Grama, nor to the rest of Mama's family. They had been brought up right, most of them belonged to the Woman's Christian Temperance Union (W.C.T.U.), and they knew what the Drink could do—they'd heard what could happen when old John Barleycorn got you in his power. So the still had to be carefully hidden from Mama's large, friendly family as well as from the rest of the world.

By this time, it was the end of November and a little quiet moonshining was about the only work Mama could do. She was enjoying being pregnant, but her doctor had forbidden her to gain any more than ten pounds, so about this time the strain of living on grapefruit and eggs was beginning to tell. Mama and Daddy were both under terrible tension about owing so much money, but at least Daddy was eating well. He tried to minimize the danger, pointing out the perfect seclusion of the spot, and the fact that they'd lived there for years—peaceable, law-abiding folks who never made any trouble. But just the same, Mama felt she was sitting on a loaded time bomb. Her whole life was holding its breath . . .waiting. She was waiting to have a baby, waiting for the first batch of whisky to come of age, waiting for prosperity (just around the corner, they kept saying), and always, always waiting for someone to discover the terrible Rose.

Rose, however, was of sterner stuff, and wasted no time on worrying and waiting. The gauges on the first six barrels of mash registered the magic figure, and Daddy drained the liquid off the bottom of the barrels, through the copper spigots, and into the huge copper vat over the distillate burner. The gentle fire simmered the juicy stuff slowly and the steam hissed up into Rose's innards. Here she gurgled and clinked and spluttered merrily until the first diamonds sprinkled unto the first fifty-gallon barrel. It took surprisingly little time to fill the bottom of the big wooden cask with this stuff that looked like water. It was four in the morning when the first moonshine was born, and they called Roger at seven to sample the first run. He rolled the stuff over his tongue, swallowed slowly, and shook all over once.

"Say, this is top-grade stuff, Jack!" he crowed. "No rotgut from our Rose. I bet if we're willing to age it, we can get ten dollars a gallon instead of the usual eight!"

Jack and Roger and Mama were as thrilled as children, and all three of them fell to plotting and figuring their profits like a pack of mad geniuses, right there on the barn floor by the glow of Rose's subtle firelight. It was just beginning to get light and the poor chickens were completely unnerved. They wouldn't even cackle, but just sat on their roosts and sulked. Mama lifted the morning's supply of still-warm eggs out from under the outraged hens, and went in to make a gay celebration breakfast. And while they raved and plotted and surmised, gentle Rose modestly plinked and trickled, steadfast and true. When they came back to the barn an hour later, the first barrel was almost half full. They were on their way to riches—wealth! Even Mama stopped worrying, while they all scampered to keep barrels and tops to nail on ready, as Rose gurgled steadily through the day. First one fifty-gallon barrel was full, and then the second, and by the next afternoon when Roger returned with the six storage barrels, three hundred gallons were finished and ready to "age." (For a week, if they could stand the wait.)

The following week Roger rolled away, the Dodge loaded to the ceiling, thanks to the window shades, with real, aged-in-the-wood, sour-mash corn liquor. Late that evening he brought back $450. The blind pigs were delighted, and soon the word spread that Anderson was really getting ahold of good stuff—"aged, ya know!"

By the middle of December 1929, the Palmer Moonshine Company was in full swing, making $100 a day when $15 a week was a good wage. The whole world sang:

> *I'd sell my shoes*
> *For a bottle of booze!*
> *Nobody knows,*
> *How dry I am!*

Mama and Daddy were doing their best to help them out.

CHAPTER 3

The moonshining went along as smooth as sin.

"Too damn smooth," complained Daddy. "It just can't be this easy to make seven hundred dollars a week! It's like the Lake when it's too calm and glassy—you know something is going to happen!"

But nothing did happen. Rose produced without faltering, day after day. Roger rumbled the Dodge into the barn about every other evening, and his only regret was that they couldn't make more than they did. The chickens got used to Jack and didn't complain any more. Even the weather helped to hide the operations perfectly. The sky was thick gray, full of that soft, thin drizzle that is Seattle in the winter. It got dark about four thirty in the afternoon, and it was often foggy. The laden Dodge was a ghost car that no one ever saw come or go. The days were cold and miserable, so there were no curious neighbors out for a walk. Yet the nights were never so cold that Jack had to worry about the water pipes to the barn freezing.

As Dad became more adept, as he tinkered and puttered with all the gadgets and knobs and tubes, he was able to turn out even more whisky every day. So it wasn't until Christmas Eve that he decided to give Rose a rest. He turned the oil burner on very low so the mash would remain constant instead of fermenting further, and let the last few drops dribble from the copper spigot. The chickens talked among themselves, settled down further into their feathers, and closed their eyes. Mama said they both realized when they turned the thing off that they hadn't really known peace of mind since they'd started the still. When the fire was out and the tubes stopped dripping, it was like a fever lifting. Neither one of them made a very good lawbreaker; no matter how they rationalized about a bad law and good intentions. It was very good not to have a crime going on in the barn on Christmas Eve.

Christmas day was fine, cold and clear. Everyone was starved to see the sun, and there it was, like a Christmas present. Grama and all the Zeller family came for Christmas dinner. They came in carloads as soon as church let out—uncles and aunts, cousins, nieces and nephews, children and babies and mamas. The children pranced and frisked outside, and Grandpa Zeller found pennies behind his ear for all of them. The women all helped out in the kitchen to fix the spread, and told each other how it was when they had their last baby and who was going to have the next one, as the men talked like men in the living room.

At dinnertime the red-cheeked children were called in, the men put out their cigars and took off their suit coats, the ladies their aprons, and they sat down to eat. Grandpa said Grace, and at "Amen" the family of good scoffers went to work on five young hens who had given their all for the occasion. They pushed the depression out the back door for a little while and drowned their sorrows in fried chicken, giblet gravy, whipped potatoes, candied sweet potatoes, buttered peas and carrots, fruit salad with whipped cream, shrimp and crab salad, homemade rolls, olives, dill pickles and celery. Everyone talked and laughed and ate at the big table, while the children had contests at the card tables in the living room to see who could eat the most olives.

"Mince or punkin', take your choice," said Mama offering the tray of homemade pies that Grama had brought.

The afternoon changed slowly into evening. The babies were put down for naps and wakened. The little girls tittered as they tried on the ladies' hats in the bedroom, and the boys grew more boisterous and quarrelsome. The women fixed another pot of coffee and set out the remains of the pies and fruitcake, and finally it was time to go home. The house was empty and still as Mama cleaned the ash trays and put the coffee cups in the sink.

"This has been one hell of a year, hasn't it, kid?" said Daddy. "But just you wait and see. We'll have everybody paid off by the time the baby is born, and we can get rid of that mess in the barn. Just wait and see, Alice; 1930 is going to be a lulu!"

It was about two weeks after Christmas 1930, when Jack paid off the last $200 owing to Gust Swensen, the painter on the Capitol View Apartments. Gust was a bachelor who lived in a downtown apartment hotel, so he was glad to come out to the ranch for a day of fresh air and one of Mama's home cooked dinners. He always brought his Shorty with him, a fat droopy-eyed basset, and Gust's only love.

Roger Anderson had been there early that Sunday morning and left a $450 payment for a Saturday night delivery. As soon as he left, Daddy called Gust. "I've got the rest of that money for you, Gust," he said triumphantly. "You better come out and plan to spend the day. Sure, sure, Gust. Bring Shorty along. We'd love to see her."

Mama put the coffee pot on and found some lump sugar for Gust. He called it *Klumpsukkerr* and liked to hold it on his tongue while he drank his coffee. Shorty liked a few lumps to nibble on, too. Since paying off a debt was always a cause for celebration, Mama sliced some fresh bread and opened the last jar of wild blackberry jam that Grama had left. Grama has the touch with wild blackberries and can turn them into pure essence of summertime to be ladled onto toast in the chill of winter. She had just eased the ruby globe of jelly into the little crystal dish, when Gust and Shorty arrived.

Gust shook hands in his great, booming Swede way, while Shorty delicately offered up a paw to Mama and Daddy and then to Gust. The formalities over with, she walked solemnly into the kitchen and sat down by the table, trying to be casual about the toast and jelly laid out. Gust was overflowing with good spirits as he said, "She's always hungry these days. Shorty's in the family way, you know." No expectant father could have been more proud, yet modest; delighted, yet a little harassed at the charming vagaries of women.

"All this time we wanted puppies, but nothing doing. Now just when I need the money so bad, and we live in such a coop in that hotel, now she has puppies!" he said, laughing.

Jack commiserated with Gust about the problems of family men and flighty women while Shorty and Mama had another piece of bread and jelly. After they finished the coffee, Gust insisted on chopping some wood for the fireplace. "We would sure not want the little mothers to take cold. I just chop for the day. This thing I like to do, you know. I feel like a boy in the old country again."

It had snowed the night before and instead of its melting to an ugly slush, the weather remained cold and dry. Just the few inches of snow was enough to cover the dead grass and Mama said she felt very cozy and safe sitting by the fireplace, looking out on the white, clean world. Even a little snow, when it sticks, is enough to snarl traffic to a standstill in Seattle. People look at it in surprise, and are likely to stay at home if at all possible and talk of the bad winters in years past. "Like that winter in 'twenty-four when we had seven inches!" Sumerville Street was a very steep, unpaved hill then, so they were practically invulnerable. Even Daddy felt quite relaxed about the still, and they both hoped the snow would last a long time.

After Gust brought the great armload of wood, he sat down in the rocker to smoke. Shorty thumped her tail for a while, and then nuzzled her head deeper between her paws to sleep. But Gust couldn't sit still. He stood up, relit his pipe and cleared his throat. He seemed so ill at ease and embarrassed that Mama went out to the kitchen to put the roast on, thinking perhaps he had some man thing to discuss with Jack.

Finally it came out. It seemed that Gust was having some prohibition problems of his own. "A painter, you know—well, it's the fumes, I guess. Them damn fumes, they just choke you up something terrible. And at night when I get home from painting all day, I kind of like to have a little something to drink, maybe a couple of drinks. But this bootleg stuff . . . you know, Jack, it's no good. I can't afford any way. So, I make myself a little rig like we used to have on the farm at home. A teakettle still I think you call it. It works just so good. But that landlady, that Kalvorsen, she has a nose like a hound. She sniffs at Shorty and me like we been washing our hair in the stuff. Now a little sniffing I can stand, but Jack, the woman is a good cook! She makes the best lutfisk in town and she takes care of Shorty if I work. So I figger I got to get rid of that teakettle still."

"And I was thinking . . . well, you folks live so far out and all. Now Missus, you just say right out if you don't like it. But I thought maybe I leave the little still here on your back porch. It wouldn't be any trouble to you, and Shorty and I could come out and make a little batch whenever we need some."

Jack assured Gust it would be perfectly all right to leave his teakettle and come and get some whenever he wanted to. Gust brought in his tempest in a copper teapot, set the thing up on the back porch, and explained in detail and slowly how it worked. It was a Rube Goldberg kind of a thing made from an ordinary copper teakettle. As the mixture in the pot boiled, the steam from the spout was led through a tiny coil, and cooled by water poured on by hand.

"And if you ever think there's going to be any trouble about it, anybody looking around or anything, you know you just call me and I take all the blame!" Gust said on leaving.

CHAPTER 4

Gust was even a poorer crook than Mama and Daddy. He and Shorty always slunk out of his old car, glancing furtively over their shoulders, as if they were running a counterfeiting ring out there on the back porch instead of making a cupful of redeye. He was careful to phone to be sure the Palmers didn't have company, and that he wouldn't inconvenience them, but one morning about the middle of January they saw his ancient car sliding down Sumerville Street unannounced.

"Those paint fumes must really be bad this morning!" laughed Daddy. "He's going like a bat out of hell!"

The light snow still covered the countryside and had turned to dirty ice on the roads, but Gust drove down the street at full tilt. "I'm going to Alaska, Jack! Ya, a job I got there waiting for me. The brother-in-law of Mrs. Kalvorsen was down to the apartment last night looking for a painter to do a cannery job in Ketchikan, but I got to be on the boat by three tomorrow afternoon!"

"Why Gust," Mama protested, "How can they possibly expect you to be ready that soon? You'll need warm clothing and equipment for the job. And how about your apartment, your furniture? And Shorty, what about Shorty?"

"I tell you, Missus, if I'm not ready by three tomorrow afternoon, there's maybe twenty men who will be! Brita, Mrs. Kalvorsen, will store my things here till I get back. I owe her rent anyway for two months. I don't work more than five or six days since we finish the Capitol View. I owed all the two hundred dollars you are paying me to General Paint. Ya, that and a little more any way.

"I would take that job if it was last night even. Right now I go to sell my brushes and ladders so I can buy some cold weather outfits from Alaska Supply. But Kalvorsen says the paint and supplies are already there on the job anyway. But Missus, Shorty is the one, I can't . . ."

Mama could see that Gust was having a hard time talking.

"I can't take her on the boat. The puppies will come very soon now. There would be no place on the boat for her. No place up there either. I can't leave her with Brita—she's got all those wild children running around. Shorty's always lived so quiet you know." The dog knew her friend was in trouble, and solemnly offered her paw to him to shake. This was too much for Gust to stand. He lifted the great homely thing up in his arms and stomped out the front door, choking.

"Tell him we'll take her, Jack," said Mama. "We'll keep Shorty, and the puppies too, until he gets back."

By this time she was almost crying too, and Gust didn't even dare say good-by. Mama took the heavy dog out of his arms into her own. "We'll take good care of her, Gust. Don't worry. Just write and tell us where you are and we'll keep in touch."

"Better hurry, Gust," said Jack, hustling him to his car. "You've still got to get those clothes. Write real soon and tell us about Ketchikan."

"She likes a little *Klumpsukker*r when she feels blue," Gust said. He got into the car and drove off looking very sternly ahead. Shorty and Mama went in to have another cup of coffee and a little *Klumpsukkerr*.

The days that followed Gust's departure were pleasant and full of pale winter sunshine, but still very cold. Just as the thin film of snow became slightly soiled and worn out, another powdery covering would come down to freshen the earth. The sun on the snow reflected in the windows and lit up the house. Jack was busy keeping Rose warm and running smoothly, while Shorty and Mama settled down seriously to hatching their young. It was too late by then to worry about gaining weight, so they nibbled when they felt like it and each took a long nap every day.

Shorty had no idea that she was a dog. Gust had never treated her like one, so she made a charming companion. Jack fixed a cardboard box lined with old woolen blankets under the stove in the kitchen for her and the family, and she moved in to wait as if she'd always been there, and drowsed contentedly by the fireplace while Mama read or played cribbage with Daddy in the evening. Sometimes they made popcorn, and Shorty always had her own plate full. She would lip up each kernel and carefully chew it with her small front teeth, looking very reproachful if it was not buttered.

When Shorty's time came, it was in the middle of the night, of course. Mama could hear the dog's toenails clicking on the linoleum as Shorty paced slowly around the kitchen, and when she saw the dog she knew the puppies would be born soon. Shorty went about the business of bringing her babies into the world as easily and competently as if it were her tenth litter instead of her first. She sniffed and snipped and licked the tiny, mouselike dogs- first one, then three more, and then after a short rest, perfect twins were born together.

"And when she calmly proceeded to have six more puppies, I couldn't believe my eyes!" said Mama later. "It began to look like a joke someone was playing on me. The book on bassets promised only three or four in the first litter, and here they were, just tumbling out, one after the other!"

She said she dashed in to tell Daddy, but he only accused her of being overwrought and said she was exaggerating as usual, and he turned over and went back to sleep, as usual.

"Well, I don't mind telling you, I was panic-stricken at this point," admitted Mama. "I knew that Shorty simply did not have the facilities to feed all those puppies. I counted them again to be sure. Twelve—one even dozen!"

But Shorty didn't seem to realize that she had confounded the basset book. She cleaned each sleek little body with the aplomb of a head nurse, and calmly stowed all twelve of them neatly into the blanket-lined box under the stove, then settled herself carefully and nudged them together for their first breakfast. They simply had to take turns.

MAMA AND DADDY SLEPT TILL almost nine that next morning, when Shorty padded in to remind them that, after all, they did have a family to think about now, and considerable changes would have to be made in the routine of the household. No more of this lolling in bed till all hours. They both rushed in to see how the babies had survived their first night, only to find all twelve of them mewing pitifully and all trying to suck each other's paws and tails and ears. Mama fixed a large egg nog affair for Shorty, while Dad marveled over the satin-coated puppies.

"Eight girls and four boys! Just wait till we write Gust. He'll have to buy out every cigar store in Ketchikan!"

By the time the puppies got their eyes open, Shorty had them all as fat as little sausages. Mama tried to convince them their box was the world, but they soon found that the most interesting smells and sounds and flavors were to be found outside the cardboard walls. Soon they were slipping over the linoleum floors, wrestling and boxing each other until both Shorty and Mama were frantic. It was still too cold to put them outside, but finally Mama thought of moving the whole family out to the barn with Rose.

"Damn it, an honest bootlegger can't even make a good batch of moon these days without twenty chickens and thirteen dogs looking over his shoulder and under his feet," huffed Daddy, who felt that all this biology business was ganging up on him somehow.

Just the same, Shorty and the "kids" moved in, and right from the first night they were happy with their new apartment. The little dogs were fascinated by the light from the fire, and the gurgling noises that Rose made were like a lullaby.

CHAPTER 5

The morning of January 28, 1930, was very cold and dry. It was just beginning to get light when Daddy finished his coffee and went out to the barn to start the next vat of whisky. He'd been gone about an hour, long enough to drain off the mash, pour it into the cooking vat, and heat up the fire, when he came into the house.

"It's too damn cold out there!" he said, stamping the snow off his boots, and clapping his hands together to get them warm. "I don't like the way Rose is acting. I don't seem to have enough water pressure for the cooling apparatus around the coils. I'll keep my eye on things out there, but you'd better take a walk up to Rainier Avenue and see what gives with the water main. Maybe they're working on it."

He added another coat and tied a scarf over his head and ears, and stomped out again. Shorty had the pups out for some fresh air and shadow-chasing, and when she saw Mama putting on her boots and coat, she was all ready for a romp in the snow.

Mama was sure that Daddy was merely fiddling and fussing over nothing. He was probably just tired and nervous, but she felt the walk would do her good anyway. She had to laugh at her reflection in the mirror as she went outside. Her old coat was straining at every button, and a soft cloche pulled down over her ears added to the pear-shaped effect.

It had not snowed for several days and the last layer had melted and refrozen to a thin glaze of ice, but going uphill there was little danger of slipping. Mama walked very slowly, waddling slightly, and was glad to see that there was no one to watch her inching up the hill. She wished she had brought some crumbs for the sparrows, as the snow had covered their food supply for almost three weeks . . . then she saw the water. The main pipe at the top of the hill was gushing water six feet into the air. A dirty finger of water reached down the hill toward her.

She knew instantly that this was what Daddy feared as the worst thing that could happen. He had the oil fire under the still turned at the highest temperature to heat the vat of new mash, and the water around the steam coils was the only cooling agent that kept the whole thing from exploding. Now, in a very few minutes, that water would be gone. She shouted and waved as she scrambled down the steep, icy street, and caught herself just in time as she started to fall.

The water ran down ahead of her as if it were racing her to destroy the barn and Daddy in it. She was clumsy and heavy, which made hurrying down the hill impossible. Again and again she forced herself to walk slowly, carefully, watching every step, when she wanted to run, gallop, to fly to the barn.

At last she reached the bottom of the icy hill, hurried across the little valley, and started up the rise to the house. She could walk faster then as the danger of slipping was less, but as she quickened her steps, her heart felt as though it were coming loose inside.

Mama was about a hundred feet from the old barn when a column of flame blasted the whole roof from the building. The explosion knocked her to the ground, and when she got up, the air around her was filled with shingles, boards, chicken feathers and burning brands of wood. The next belch of noise pushed out the windows and front door, with Daddy right behind it. His body lay face down, flat on the large barn door, about fifteen feet from the furnace that used to be the barn.

Mama grabbed his feet and dragged him toward the house, but he was too heavy. When she rolled him over on his back, the whole front of him was soot black.

"I knew then that he was dead," said Mama, "but even with a corpse on my hands, I took my coat and rubbed the oil and dirt off his face. He opened those white eyeballs and yelled like a wild man as I brushed his face. And when he sat up, it was as amazing as if it were the Resurrection right there on Sumerville Street!"

Somehow Daddy got to his feet and Mama helped him into the house. She rubbed cold cream on his face and arms while he phoned Roger Anderson.

"What time is it, Jack?" asked Mama, as he hung up.

"About nine, I guess. Roger's calling Sergeant Wattler, Alice. They'll have a couple of cops out here to see that nothing goes wrong, that nobody takes anything, and we'll stay at Roger's place till everything blows over. He says Wattler knows what to do. He knows the boys in the fire department, so no one will know a thing about the explosion. Just don't get excited, kid. Throw a few things in a bag and we'll be ready to go when Roger gets here."

"O.K., Jack. We'll be ready. You get Shorty and the pups while I pack. Say, what time do you have now?" she asked. When Roger arrived about a half hour later, the flames were still crackling and Mama was still throwing things in the bag.

"What in hell are you doing, Alice? We'll only be gone a few days. You've got enough stuff in there for a trip to Timbuktu!" growled Daddy.

"I'm sorry, Jack, but you'll have to drop me off at the hospital. I'm going to have a baby," Mama told him, trying to sound calm.

All through the fire, and catching the puppies, and packing, Dad had remained firm and cool, but at that point he went to pieces. "Jesus Christ! This is the last straw," he moaned. "You're going to have a baby? Now?"

Even through the soot on his face, he looked pale enough to faint. Roger took one arm and Mama took the other and they lifted him into the car, along with three suitcases, Shorty, and twelve squealing, squirming little puppies.

As they drove away up Sumerville Street, the fire engine passed them, speeding toward the barn, which was blazing away like a neon sign advertising the fact that the Palmers were running a still. When Roger eased the big car into the receiving entrance of Providence Hospital, they left Daddy shaken and muttering to himself, like a man who has been deeply wronged. While Roger helped Mama into the hospital, Shorty and each one of the pups howled at a different vantage point inside the car.

For all Mama knew the barn and Rose were still burning. But for a little while, they would all have to wait—Mama was having a baby. The Providence Hospital delivery room closed its shining white walls peacefully around her.

But that evening Daddy and reality came in together during visiting hours. "The poor little kid. She looks just like me!" he said. "And she's bald as an egg, kind of like my old man before he died."

"Of course she looks like you," said Mama. "But she's a beautiful child. Even the nurse says so!"

"Well sure, Alice, she's fine. They say they always look better in a couple of weeks," Daddy allowed. "Now, your ma is going to stay out at the ranch with us for a few weeks after you get home. She can help out until you're on your feet again. She's down the hall now, looking at the baby. I was out home this afternoon and everything is fine . . . not a thing to worry about. Wattler has a couple of cops out there until I get back tonight. I'm going to pick up Roger on the way home and he's going to help clean up the mess. So you just relax."

"But Jack, what about Rose? There must be enough left so people can't help knowing. What did the neighbors think? What did the firemen say? . . . And the woman with the birth certificate says I have to have a name ready or they'll call her Baby Palmer."

"Well hell, Alice. This was all your idea anyway. I haven't even considered any girls' names."

Mama rose above this slur with, "I read a lovely story once about a Lady Artis, an English noblewoman who kept peacocks and everything. How does Artis sound to you?"

"Just swell," agreed Daddy. "Everyone's convinced we're nuts by this time, anyway. 'Artis' will be fine. Don't worry about a thing. I'll see you tomorrow."

After the two weeks of flat-on-your-back bed rest that was the fashion in the maternity ward in those days, Mama was weak and useless by the time she was ready to go home. Her legs had forgotten how to walk and her muscles thought she had died two weeks before. But with the aid of a wheel chair and Roger Anderson's town Packard, we made it home. Everyone carefully avoided looking in the direction of the barn. But it was there anyway. Rather, what was left of it was there. Dad and Roger had cleared away the rubble, and they'd built a small coop for a new generation of chickens.

Grama met us at the front door and Mama could tell that a new era had been established. The windows shone, and the whole house smacked of a good airing. The sheets on the bed, cool and smelling of wind, were turned back, and the pillows were plumped up. Mama felt as wobbly as a thin layer of gelatin lying there, but Grama took over. She wasn't hampered by the inhuman child-bearing practices of the thirties, so they had very little trouble with me.

Sara Zeller was the oldest of a family of eleven children, all born and brought up on a lonely Minnesota farm, so babies were an old, old story to her, although she still had very definite ideas on the science of the subject. "In my day," said Grama, "we didn't talk about having babies. We just had 'em." She was even too delicate to refer to a mother dog as "she." With Grama it was always: "*He* had puppies."

Aunt Esther and all of Mama's cousins and friends discussed and argued, worried and read books, but Grama just calmly went her own way. She'd never heard of Freud and always had her babies "broke" by the time they were a year old, but she would no more let a child's cry go unanswered than she would forget to say her prayers or to wear her W.C.T.U. pin on her good black coat on Sundays.

No hurt knee or insulted pride was so bad that it couldn't be made to feel better on Grama's lap. She'd dig into her cache and find a peppermint, or a crisp apple to peel, or a picture of a kitten to cut out of the *Ladies' Home Journal*. She could mend doll heads broken too badly for anyone else to bother with. Or when a youngster had been ornery all day until everyone was sore and out of patience, Grama could lure him to her room to cut out strings of paper dolls, or to watch her make funny shadows on the walls with her big-knuckled old hands. Finally, out would come a charming mild child, and everyone would wonder how they could have been so hard on the little sweetheart.

So, when Mama handed me over to Grama, there was no nervous fluster of sterilizing bottles, agonizing over just the right feeding schedule, and staying awake while the baby cried at night. "I don't hold none with this nonsense about a baby crying to develop its lungs. Plenty of time for the little darlings to develop their lungs by just plain breathing." Grama just mixed a little boiled water and sugar with milk for the bottle, cuddled the baby into her own bed, and announced, "My babies never cry." They never did, either.

Mama had been home about a week when Roger dropped out to the house for a conference and insisted on giving them the payment for the last whisky they'd made without taking his cut. "Kind of a baby present," he called it.

"Old Wattler has been calling twice a day since the fire, trying to line up a new location for us, but I told him I'd have to talk to you folks first, Jack. He's even willing to finance a new barn for you and pay for the equipment for a new still. He's such a crook, though. I kind of hate to get mixed up with him again."

"Roger, it isn't the rebuilding or the money or anything like that," answered Mama. "But Jack and I have talked it over a dozen times and a dozen ways. And as badly as we need the money, we can't go back in with you. It's the baby, that's all. She's too little and helpless. What would happen to her if anything went wrong?"

The folks didn't see Roger Anderson again. He said he would stay away from them until the Federal Agents stopped checking so closely on him, but several months later Daddy heard through a mutual friend that Roger was in prison. They'd caught him loading moonshine into the old Dodge over in the Ballard district. Two brothers, Terry and Ben O'Moore, were involved in the arrest, too. It was in their store that the still was located, but Roger insisted he was renting the building and that the O'Moore boys knew nothing of his activities.

"He was the nicest bootlegger we ever knew," said Mama. "I was always sorry that we hadn't asked him to be godfather to Artis."

I was only about five weeks old when Aunt Lilly called Mama about going to work. "This is Lillian, Alice. (She always called herself Lillian. She hated the name Lilly and we only called her that when she was well out of range.) We heard you had a little trouble out at the ranch, but if it's all over now, we'd like to have you come out to the store and help us out. We need a book-keeper, and it would be a job where you could be sitting down most of the time. Talk it over with Jack, and if Sara can take care of the baby, let me know."

Of course, Grama, who had taken over as permanent baby-sitter, was delighted to have Mama out of the way, and I was her special pet from that day on. Mama started at seventeen dollars a week at Zeller's Grocery in Normandy Park, with ten per cent off on the food bill.

By this time Grama and the rest of the family all knew what had happened, but not one of them ever spoke one word of it to each other or to anyone else. Grama's sisters could deliver vehement sermons on child-rearing if one of the youngsters was "fresh," and they would gossip enthusiastically about "Maysie's girl marrying that sailor, and her knowing him only just the two weeks!" But when we got into real trouble, then they were an organized front.

"No use talking about something that's well over and done with!" said Aunt Lilly. So Rose was a chapter that was finished.

CHAPTER 6

During the early months of 1930, on the financial page of the Seattle *Post-Intelligencer* it said, "American business is willing to turn its back on this past year. It already has written off the experience as painful perhaps, but salutary. Now it is turning its eyes forward to another era of improvement which may carry this nation, and with it, the world, to new heights of achievement and prosperity!"

In the meantime, Daddy shrank a little more each day while he sat and waited. Mama's wages went down to $13.50 and finally down to $12.00 a week, when Daddy was called in by the King County Relief Commission to do "Maintenance Work" at Seward Park. Maintenance work turned out to be raking leaves and debris left by picnickers. The men would gather the leaves into neat piles and then, while they stood on one foot and leaned against their rakes, the foreman would rake all the piles together and burn them. Daddy stayed on the list for almost two months, working three days a week, until somehow the Commission found that his wife was working.

When they dropped him, Daddy admitted, "It was three days' work a week, but you know it's a hell of a relief not to have to stand in the park waiting for the next leaf to fall. There we'd be, twenty or thirty big, husky guys, carpenters and bookkeepers, truck drivers and mechanics, raking those damn leaves and little bits of papers from one side of the park to the other till we had them just about worn thin. The foreman of our gang—he was the one who handed out the rakes and kept our time—he was one of the chief engineers on the Aurora Bridge!"

But Portland had the answer. The headlines said: "Unemployment Problem in Portland Largely Solved! Jobs for Two Thousand Men Found by Public-Spirited Citizens!" It turned out that the public-spirited citizens put two thousand men to work for a couple of weeks doing odd jobs, yard work and heavy housecleaning. What they did after the two weeks were over, the article didn't say.

That was the spring Daddy decided to plant a garden. He didn't have anything else to do and he thought perhaps he would be able to sell some of the produce. Grama had kept chickens out in back of the house for years, and the soil was black and rich. The corn seed had only been in the ground a few days when the first curling shoots stuck their heads up, and the Chinese pheasants were out early every morning to eat them. Grama made a sleazy looking scarecrow out of a pair of old overalls that flapped in the wind, but no one was fooled. The robins even sat on his hat and squawked at us.

But before the second planting of corn was up, Daddy had become an excellent shot. The fat hens and showy roosters would poke along out of the high grass, so slowly and gradually that they seemed to appear out of nowhere. Then, just as slowly, Daddy would lift the gun, take aim, and Ka-pow! The beautiful bird would splutter into the soft earth, and lie still.

At first, Dad was lucky to get even a body shot, and Grama would have to pick buckshot for hours before the bird was fit to eat. But before the corn was up, he almost always killed with a head shot. So, while food columnists recommended special economy meals for the "Elastic Budget," the Palmers dined on breast of pheasant, fried pheasant with garlic and rosemary, and pheasant with rice and mushrooms. (When the mushrooms at Aunt Lilly's store got brown, they were discarded, so we had them often.)

But by June the garden was well on its way, there weren't any more pheasants to shoot, and the men just sat. They studied the Townsend Plan, and some of them joined the "Apple Army" that marched on the White House to camp on the lawn for a few weeks to demand their army bonuses. But then, when nothing happened, they marched home again, and things were still the same.

IT WAS THAT SAME SUMMER that Old Man Schimmel tried to sell Uncle Max his Ford. Mr. Schimmel was an old friend of Grama's who had gone to mission with her and Grandpa since they first came to Seattle in 1890. He had a little hardware store next to a bakery on 18th and Yesler, and never did make very much . . . just enough to get by. Even in good times, old Schimmel wasn't a successful businessman. He always trusted people too much, and gave too many sacks of nails away to little boys with projects. But that summer when he offered Max his old car for twenty-five dollars, Mama said she noticed how thin and old he looked. At the time Max was raising chickens and selling the eggs, and could have put the car to good use on his delivery route, but he was hard-up too.

"I'm sure sorry, Mr. Schimmel. I could really use that car, but I just can't see my way clear to buy it. I'd like to take it off your hands, but the egg business isn't so hot right now. Have you tried Uncle Ludwig?"

"Oh, I think not, Maxie. Ludwig's got a fine car already. But don't you worry about it. I'll just have to work it out some other way. Say hello to your mama for me."

It was only about a week later when Max and Daddy dropped over to the old man's little store. It was Sunday and the front door was locked, but he always left the back door open. They thought he must be asleep when no one answered the knock, so they walked in. But old man Schimmel wasn't asleep. The smell of gas was still strong in the clean back room, and he was lying on the narrow cot by the stove, his shoes placed neatly on the floor. He didn't leave a note—I guess he didn't have anyone to leave one for. But there, leaning against the alarm clock on the table, was a neat new registration card for his old Ford, made out to Max Wilhelm Zeller.

Still, it was called only a temporary recession. The headlines read, "Trade, Industry and Commerce Surge Forward in the Pacific

Northwest!" But on the next page, the want ads were enough to make a man cry. Under "Men Wanted" there was the most fantastic collection of pipe dreams and phony schemes imaginable.

Reliable go-getter to sell copper mine stock. $20,000 guaranteed first year.

Enroll now at the Acme Barber College. Superb salary forthcoming. Pay a little down, a little each month. Invisible hair-net menders urgently needed, today! Fantastic commission on piece work!

While on the other side of the page, the columns were full of stores for sale—cheap. Lots for sale. Tools for sale. Clothes for sale. Souls and hearts and pride . . . for sale, cheap!

In the meantime, while the men sat and waited, they talked and grumbled and griped and thought up wild schemes to make money. Some of them were so wild that they actually worked. Somebody thought of golf for poor men—miniature golf, and for a while it was the rage.

One crackpot even tried to talk Daddy into building some crazy little wooden gambling machines. Mr. Bernstein explained that the idea of the thing was for the player to insert a nickel in the slot. The coin set off a metal ball, magnetically controlled to win only a small percentage of the time. If the ball went into the winner's slot, several previously played coins would pour out into the player's lap. He said if Daddy would build twenty of his machines, he could have half interest in all profits made. Mama said they did their best not to laugh in his face while the earnest little man explained his invention, and they eased him out as kindly as possible. They had a good laugh about the poor fool when he left—a pinball machine, he called it.

That was also the summer that the Palmers went on relief. Grama told about the time of the drought when she was a little girl on the farm in Minnesota when they ate an awful lot of potatoes, but they never had to ask for charity. And about the time when the grasshoppers ate everything but the beans, and her mother learned to make bread out of beans instead of wheat. But no one in our family, as far back as Grama could remember, had ever had to ask for help.

The district office was down in Columbia City, so Daddy usually walked down to pick up the stamps to be cashed for a week's supply of food. Mama could always tell when he'd been down there. He was sore and cranky and sarcastic, until it finally wore off.

"Well God dammit, Alice, I don't want a hand-out. I want a chance to go to work. We've got to *do* something. If you've got any ideas, for God's sake, let me know!"

But Mama didn't have any ideas. Neither did President Hoover, except to cut Government spending and to balance the budget. As for the Palmers, they didn't give a damn about the budget. They only knew that there must be work to be done somewhere, and they wanted a chance to do it.

"Ordinary people like us didn't go to Communist meetings or take up Technocracy," Mama explains now. "But we were exhausted and confused—we felt that somehow we had failed and didn't know where to start to pick ourselves up again. And of course, 1930 was only the beginning. By 1932 there were a lot of Democrats.

"Maybe the New Deal was just another politician's pipe dream, but at least it was something new. The following March when Roosevelt took office, we were all listening to his speech on the radio. I can remember it like it was yesterday. He admitted it, he came right out loud and said the bad word 'depression.' In fact I think he called it a grave national crisis, and then he said that the only thing we had to fear was fear itself."

But Uncle Max, who was a retired Navy chief, remained true to the Grand Old Party to the end. Straight through the "first hundred days" he snorted continually, "Why Alice, that swab is gonna be just like all the rest of those sweet-talking sons a seacooks! Wait and see!"

CHAPTER 7

The early morning fog still cooled the countryside and promised a fine warm day on June 15, 1934. Dad was putting some new fire brick in one of Aunt Ganelle's houses in West Seattle, and the job was almost finished. The house was near Alki Beach on Puget Sound, so Mama had planned to take Grama and me to spend the day at the water while he worked. She had packed the big old picnic basket with enough lunch for Daddy, too, and was gathering up the suntan lotion, towels, and a bathing suit for everyone, when the phone rang.

"Get it, will you, Jack? I've got my hands full."

"Hello . . . Well, welcome home, stranger! Alice, it's Gust. He's in Seattle.

"We were just talking about you the other day, Gust. Wondering what you were doing and how you like Alaska and everything. Haven't heard a word from you since we sent Shorty and the pups to your sister, and we. . . ."

"Well, sure I need a job. Hell, who doesn't? We haven't really done anything for almost three years now . . . Where? Nome, Alaska? Where's that? . . . Well, I'll tell you, Gust, we'll talk it over and I'll call you back tomorrow morning . . . Oh, I see. O.K., I'll call you right back then. Yeah, MAin 2778.

"Alice, it's a job! A steady job for four months. Some kind of a mining company that Gust worked for last summer. He says since they revaluated the gold quite a few outfits are going in up there. They need a cat-skinner in a place called Nome, in Alaska. But that crazy Swede says I've got to be ready to go by one o'clock this afternoon. The *Victoria* leaves from Pier Two at one. Well, what do you think?"

"I just don't know what to think," said Mama weakly. "What is a cat-skinner anyway, Jack? You're not a cat-skinner! How much will they pay you? How much would the boat fare be? What kind of a mine is it? Would there be a place for us to stay and . . . ."

"How in hell do I know what a cat-skinner is? Somebody who drives a tractor, I guess. I can do it as well as the next guy, though, that's for sure. He didn't say how much, but they will pay a regular salary and the fare up and back. It's a job, Alice. That's all I know. But after rotting for three years in this lousy town, I don't think we're in any position to be picking at the little details!"

"All right, Jack. There's no need to shout. It's almost nine now. We could get Harry to finish Aunt Ganelle's fireplace. Then I think she'll pay us this morning for the job if we go right over there now and explain to her."

"O.K., Alice. I'll call Gust first and see what I'll need to take along. Just think of it, girl! A real job! I can hardly believe it!"

Mama could hardly believe it either, that in ten minutes their lives had turned a corner and started in a completely new direction. And here, at the first glimpse of a steady job they had had in four years, Mama was more afraid than she'd ever been in her life. She and Dad had been sitting still, marking time, trying to wait for it to pass for so long, that when the opportunity came to move at last, she couldn't trust the stunning good luck. It must have been something like the lethargy of people in a prison that eventually becomes like a disease.

"IT WAS AS IF JACK and I were walking along a very high, slender wire, way above the world, and one wrong move, even the wrong word whispered, would dash us both back down into the quicksand again."

By the time Uncle Max arrived at the ranch to lend them his Ford, they were both dressed and ready to go. Everything depended on getting that thirty dollars due them on the fireplace job, because Gust said that Dad would need heavy leather boots, a good sleeping bag, heavy wool pants, shirts, socks, heavy-duty wool underwear, a mackinaw, and something called "shoepacks."

When Mama told Aunt Ganelle about the plans, she was as excited as they were. "Of course you can have the thirty dollars. I'll get the cash for you right now," she said. "I always did like that brother of yours anyway, Jack. You send Harry over tomorrow to finish the fireplace and we'll call it square." Aunt Ganelle peeled off six five-dollar bills from a large roll of money she kept in a Mason jar.

"Nome, Alaska, hmm? Why boy, I've half a mind to go with you if I wasn't such an old fool. My first post when I was in the Salvation Army was in a mining town. Butte, Montana, it was. What a wonderful time we had there!"

"I'm afraid Nome would be a pretty rugged place to live, Aunt Ganelle. They say housing is . . . ."

"Housing, hah! We lived in tents for three months in Butte! Say the young folks these days have it soft. Why many's the time I was glad of my good right arm in Butte. I'm in mind of a time when a pretty young recruit and I, Sister Beulah her name was . . . well, anyway, we were selling *War Cry's* in one of the worst saloons in town. But the miners were always gentlemen when we came in, always bought a lot of *War Cry's*, and paid extra, too. When they saw the uniform they were always careful to take off their hats—respectful like, you know. But this one time when we came in, there was this young puppy standing at the end of the bar. He was quite tipsy, I'm sure, and he said something very disrespectful about Sister Beulah's blue-serge-covered bust. Well, before the bartender or the rest of the gentlemen had time to even set down their glasses to take care of him, I just put aside my *War Cry's* and tambourine, and brought one right up off the floor and flatted him, then and there. The sale afterwards on the *Cry's* was something wonderful. So, you needn't worry about me being able to take care of myself. But, I've had my turn, I guess. Time to sit back and act like an old lady."

"But now Jack, you be sure to get in touch with the Church as soon as you get in town. In those mining towns a young man needs some good firm guidance and high-type people to associate with. And I've got some of your uncle's old woolen underpants around here, if I could just think where I put them. It wouldn't take a minute to look down cellar, Alice, and there's some of those old camping outfits we used to use down at the beach."

"Well thanks, Aunt Ganelle, but we really haven't got time to wait," said Daddy. "Why don't you give Alice a call when you find them and she can mail them to me. It's ten now, and we've still got the clothes to buy before the boat leaves at one. I called Harry this morning and he'll be here early tomorrow. And thanks a lot!"

As they got into Max's old Ford, Aunt Ganelle waved her apron from the porch. "God Bless you, boy! Keep a sharp eye out for them avalanches!"

The family had always made fun of Aunt Ganelle keeping her money in the Mason jars, but now they thanked their lucky stars for her eccentricity, and then drove directly to Sears and Roebuck, where the hungry clerks waited on them as though they had three hundred dollars instead of thirty. Mama hadn't spent any money on clothes for over three years, and even the practical woolen shirts and pants were exciting to buy. But thirty dollars wouldn't stretch forever, even in 1933, so after the pants, shirts, good sleeping bag, and high leather boots, they could only allow for two pairs of beautiful red long-johns. They were finely woven, and seemed to have a warmth of their own. There were no other customers in the department that morning, so Daddy put on the lovely red underwear, and added the tall leather hiking boots for a quick waltz in front of the full-length mirrors.

"He was a miner, a forty-niner, Oh my darling Clementine! Just like a real old sourdough, hmm, kid?" he sang out to Mama.

"All right, old sourdough, we've still got to get the mackinaw and 'shoepacks,' whatever they are. The man said they might have them at Alaska Outfitting and Supply down on First Avenue. If they cost over ten dollars, you're sunk before you even get on the *Victoria*!

"Lord, why is it that men are so damnably gay when they are about to leave their homes and families for some Godforsaken hole?" mourned Mama.

At Alaska Outfitting they found an old codger who'd been dressing greenhorns for Alaska since 1906. "Yessir, been sitting on the corner here since ought-six fixin' up young fellers like you. All hot to get to Alaska for all that gold. Haw haw, most of 'em just freeze their self stiff"— and he laughed another long wicked wheeze.

"But I'll tell you folks, any mackinaws we got now run you fifteen, maybe twenty dollars, but if your poke is real low, we've got some upstairs from several years back, er . . . ah, *several* years. Just as good though, even better quality I'd say than these newer models. They knew how to make a garment in them days. I'll get one in just a jiffy here." He hopped up the stairs, still laughing a little.

Mama and Daddy poked around the stocks of pungent yellow oilskins and handmade Indian sweaters, determined not to have to admit to being complete greenhorns by asking the old man what shoepacks were. They didn't find anything that looked likely to pack into a shoe so decided to bluff it out. The little clerk came down in back of a large black object.

"Now for Nome, this here would be the ideal garment. Keep you warm as a bug in a rug. Just slip it on for size, Mr. Palmer."

The coat came almost to Dad's knees and was undeniably warm, if nothing else. It seemed to be made of several layers of coarse black plush, like the stuff they used to upholster those good durable sofas with. It buttoned from the high neck to flaring hemline in a double-breasted effect with great knobby leather buttons. It had a large cape collar of the same plush, lined with black fur seal that could be flipped up over the head and ears.

"Now there is a real mackinaw! Folks, they just don't make them that way today. On account this being your first trip and all, I'll let you have that little model for five dollars!"

"We'll think it over, but in the meantime, we will need some 'shoepacks,'" Mama said hastily, knowing she couldn't laugh.

Next the old man asked smoothly, "How many shoepacks you think you'd need, sir?"

"Oh, I guess five or six would be plenty," said Daddy carefully. "How much are they?"

At this the little demon had to lean against the counter while he howled. "Ho, five or six shoepacks, is it?" They waited while he wheezed and gasped.

"We got shoepacks all right, son, but they're just regular high leather boots with rubber feet on 'em. Double tongue, inside and out so's to keep the water out. So, unless you're hiding an extra leg or two under there, I think two of those will be enough. Hee hee, I'll get 'em. Cheap . . . only two- fifty on special now."

Dad was miffed at being found out. "About the coat, though, I don't think it's just what I was looking for. It's kind of old-fashioned looking with those leather buttons and all, and it seems awfully heavy, don't you think?"

"Too heavy? Nonsense, boy. Nome is right practical on the Arctic Circle, you know. When that wind comes in off the Bering Sea, it cuts you in half if you aren't dressed for it. But I tell you what. They made a fine hat in the fur seal to go with that number. I'll throw that in too, all for four-fifty!"

"O.K., O.K. Put it all together and we'll take it. It's almost eleven already, Alice. We haven't got time to resist."

As the old man wrapped the coat, hat and shoepacks in brown paper and twine, he questioned Daddy about the job. "What outfit you going with, Mr. Palmer? We know most everyone in Nome. Supply just about all the placer miners up there. . . .

"No, can't say as I ever heard of the Snake River Exploratory Corporation. Awful lot of new fly-by-night outfits going in there since that crazy Roosevelt brought up the value of the gold. Be lucky if you get your pay for the summer with these fly-by-night boys," he said cheerfully.

"Well folks, here's luck!" The old man slapped Daddy on the shoulders and handed him the huge package. All the way out, they could hear him cackling.

Then Daddy headed Max's Ford toward home, loaded with their purchases. "My God, Alice, look at the bulk of that damn coat. Even leaving out the sleeping bag, we'll never get the thing packed into the trunk. That old coot has probably been stuck with it since the first gold rush!"

"Never mind, Jack. They do say there is still snow up there even in June sometimes. You can use it to throw over your bunk for an extra blanket, too. And besides, only four-fifty! Why, those beautiful leather buttons alone must be worth almost that much!"

"Oh yeah, and when the Snake River Exploratory Corporation folds up and disappears, I could boil down the buttons for soup, when I'm starving out in the snow like Charlie Chaplin. That old guy never even heard of them. Do you suppose it's a fake name?"

But there was no time to worry. As soon as they got home, Mama started packing the bulky woolen clothes into one of Grama's old leather trunks. They finally jammed the last thing in and Mama sat on the bulging suitcase while Daddy fastened it. He just got the old-fashioned brass catch hooked in, when the whole thing popped open, springing the lock hopelessly. But Gram had some heavy linen twine she'd been saving for just such an occasion, so they bound the whole thing together and finished it off with big knots.

"We forgot to pack the fur hat and the shoes!" yelled Daddy. "You take the trunk out to the car and I'll get into these wool pants and shirt. I guess I'll just have to wear the shoepacks, too. They won't get lost that way. Jesus, it's hot for June! Why couldn't it rain like it always does in June? Shall we take the baby down to the boat?"

"Oh, I think not, Jack. It's almost time for her nap, and she'd only get tired and get in the way. Go ahead and get dressed and I'll load up the car."

The ride to the boat was a wild one. Through the industrial section, Mama said people were just returning to work from lunch and they seemed to dawdle at the intersections like herds of placid sheep, but Daddy managed to get to the waterfront without running any of them down. But of course, by the time they reached Pier 2, a Great Northern freight was dragging itself along Alaska Way, barring their entrance. The tail end of the train was visible about seven or eight cars down, and then finally the last link crept in front of the Ford, only to screech in agony and stop.

Finally the intricate dance of the freight cars was over. They coupled a car of mild-eyed cattle on, and trundled slowly off down Alaska Way, and Max's Ford fairly leapt over the railroad tracks and shot into the dim interior of the Pier Building.

The first and second-class passengers went on the ship from the second floor of the building, while steerage passengers and freight were stowed in from below. Gust was waiting for them just inside the building entrance. "You can park the car over on the left, Missus. Jack and I get his trunk into the hold before they close her up."

Then Gust hauled out the bulging trunk and Mama heard him say, "Yesus boy, I was beginning to think maybe you changed your mind. I was ready just about to grab one of them beauties right off Skid Road for a cat-skinner! . . . Say, that's some getup you got on, man!"

Mama found a place to park in the huge open pier building just inside the door marked "Alaska Steamship Company vehicles only. Reserved for Captain Nordby!" She set the brakes, locked the car, and ran after the two men, saying a short prayer that Captain Nordby was on the high seas.

As Dad and Gust were swallowed into the hold of the S.S. *Victoria*, Mama adjusted her eyes to the dark Pier Building to see that the ship must be in the last throes of leaving. Men shoved laden dollies in all directions, swearing at each other with enthusiasm. Several foremen stood by the great open doors of the pier, directing the loading into the hold of the ship. Mama tried to make herself very thin and out of the way, but everywhere she stepped someone was tugging, rolling, pushing, or wrestling some large pile of stuff into position for loading.

Far above, up in the sunshine, she could hear the stewards playing their chimes and calling, "All ashore's going ashore!" A stream of gay visitors filed down the gangplank. The sunshine lit their hair, and their clothes were all white with the light, and they were laughing and calling to each other. But no sunlight got down to the steerage people, below. The green-black water reflected in the high, dirty windows cast a dull gray light over all.

Dad came back over the lower gangplank. He still had on the great coat and fur hat, and looked very hot and red-faced next to the dapper Filipinos, in their beautiful hand- tailored gabardine suits, leaving to work in the fish canneries.

"Everything's put away, er . . . stowed. But dammit, it's so hot in there. And stink! Whew, now I know how the slaves must have felt!"

Gust saw Mama's stricken look and shut him up with "Now Jack, it's not near so bad once we are under way and you get that fur coat off you. The sea air makes it just so comfy as a hotel and they pay the stewards so lousy, you can buy the whole first-class kitchen for six bits from one of them."

They were watching the last small items being tucked into the hold and on spaces on the deck, when the first rumbling noise at the entrance of the pier started.

"*Ti Svolich!*" a voice boomed into the cavern of the building. "Drive this machine to the end of the pier or I kill you like a dog!" A tiny yellow tractor turned into the entrance of the pier, and the small driver hopped off, almost into the arms of the bearded man with the big voice. He danced around the big man like a fox terrier, yapping with excitement and shaking his little fists.

"You little idiot," the big bearded man started out softly, until his face was down level with the smaller man's. "Little in-fin-i-tesimal swine of a MAN!" he roared. "You think this small matter of a tractor is anything to me? Hah, it is nothing! You and it both are merely greenhorns, to me. In Russia, I would have you right here slain. As it is, you may go. I dismiss you. You will get your absurd money when my company brings out the gold in four months. If the word and sign of Count Georgi Nickolaus Barkavitch is not to be trusted then you are insane anyway, poor fellow. My best advice to you, my son, is to leap from this very pier today. Good-by, *Diavol!*"

Then he strode to the men operating the winch and demanded, "Here, boys, I have the little item of one tractor, name of Caterpillar, I believe, to be stowed under Snake River Exploratory Corporation. Please see to it at once."

So while the insulted man whimpered and tugged ineffectually at the workmen's sleeves, and they grumbled at the last-minute job, Count Barkavitch yelled the small tractor into place, calling all the workmen swine and greenhorns until his face was blue and his beautiful whiskers shook. Mama said she had the feeling he could have gotten the thing into the hold just by yelling at it, even without the winch, but at last it was safely in the steel net and placed cozily in the hold. The exasperated owner, or former owner, sank down on the piling and cried, while the Count shook hands all around and passed out enormous cigars.

"My darlings, never have I seen more beautiful stevedoring. Even in Russia this would be looked upon with admiration!" He beamed at everyone in general, and settled his own cigar and lovely brown Homburg.

"Ah, my friend Gust. I see here you have retained the cat-.skinner." He took Daddy's shoulders and smiled down at him. "Sweetheart, you look like a Mujik, but if Gust says you skin the cat, well then . . . ."

"Ah, and this is Madame the cat-skinner. My good woman, please be assured that I personally will see to it that this summer will be one of great profit for all of us. I'm delighted to make your acquaintance." His eyes swept the length of Mama's ample figure and he approved. "Such a fine, strong young woman. You could almost be Russian," he said.

"But now that the small inconvenience of the transferring of the tractor is complete, I must be getting to my cabin." Mama, Daddy, Gust, and all the laborers stood like lumps, amazed, while the fine-looking old man walked up the iron stairway that led to the upper gangplank. He strode into the sunlight and it gleamed on him, from his curling silver beard to his fine leather boots. He shouted to the head steward, "Come, darling, some of your best whisky, right away bring to my cabin. I'm expecting a Bon Voyage!"

The glow of the Count was extinguished as soon as they closed his cabin door, and the hole leading into steerage looked even darker. "O.K., boys, let's get this trap battened down," shouted one of the foremen. "Is everyone in?"

"Well, that's it, Missus," said Gust. "We be seeing you in September." He shook Mama's hand and crossed over onto the ship. They were throwing the thick lines from the ship to the men on the dock, and the huge whistle blew till her ears blew with it.

"Hurry up, Jack. They're pulling in the gangplank." Mama found that it was impossible to even kiss Daddy good-by, with all the stevedores running around and the Filipino cannery workers looking through the portholes. "Take care of yourself, Jack. Write as soon as you can and tell me what's going on, and don't worry about us."

He jumped over into the opening and they slid the metal doors shut. Then Mama saw his face again at one of the small portholes, and they both waved. They smiled and waved again, but the boat didn't move. Daddy said something but there was too much noise to hear him. Mama stood there for about ten minutes, but nothing seemed to be happening, so she sat on top of one of the pilings. The passengers on the top deck had thrown all their serpentine, and she could hear people above leaving toward the street. It was almost two o'clock when she finally made out what Dad was trying to say. "Might - as - well - go - home! Go Home!" he yelled.

"Yes," she nodded. Her smile had cracked and died long ago. "Might as well go home." The ship finally sailed about four hours later.

CHAPTER 8

Afterward, when the men talked about the trip to Nome, they always started, "Remember how we used to throw the food trays out the porthole? Just folded 'em up like a piece of cardboard, dishes and all, and dumped 'em out the window. That's the way to wash dishes!"

It seems that Gust was right when he said you could buy the whole first-class kitchen for seventy-five cents. Good food is very important on a long ocean voyage, especially when you are going by steerage and there is nothing to do. The highlight of each slow day is the meal. When it is a good meal, the day is a success, something to savor and remember and talk about. But when dinner is macaroni with stringy cheese and lumps of some anonymous kind of meat, then the day is gray, a failure. So the first thing Dad and Gust did when the boat left the silver and blue harbor was to hunt out the head steward for the steerage section.

Sure enough, he was a skinny, pale-eyed Canadian boy who looked like he didn't get enough to eat himself. They each gave him a dollar for a little something special whenever he could manage it, and he was their personal servant for the rest of the trip. Before the second day of the voyage, Red had both men comfortably settled for their meals in an empty cabin in the second-class section just at the head of the stairs leading up from steerage.

"Looks like that old couple on B Deck are going to be seasick for the whole damn trip," he told the cook in the ship's galley. "Guess I'll have to be taking trays up for them." And if the cook noticed, he must have thought that the appetite of Red's seasick old couple was amazing, because Daddy and Gust ate like kings. They chuckled and gloated over every mouthful. It was delicious food, and to add to the flavor, it was stolen and they were liable to be caught any minute.

There were few passengers on the trip, so usually the little steward had plenty of time to smuggle the trays in and out with no questions asked. But occasionally, Red was too busy to come back for the empty trays and dishes, so he left orders for Gust and Dad to "heave 'em right out the 'ole, gents. Can't have the bloody Purser finding the remains in a cabin that's supposed to be empty, you know." And heave 'em out the 'ole they did, feeling like pirates all the while.

Gust and Dad had been eating in the cabin for a full day when Red asked them if they'd mind a little company. "He's a nice chap and I'm sure you fellows can get along nicely, eh?"

Of course, they agreed and found him to be a very nice chap indeed. Kurt Nordstrom was a big Swede, about six-four, with dis-jointed-looking bones sticking out all over. He ducked his head to come into the small cabin and filled the room when he was in it. He had a shock of gray and black hair that never looked combed, and usually a couple of days' gray whiskers to match. Kurt always had so much to say, so much to laugh about, or to argue about, that he could never quite take time to finish his words. Most of his sentences ended halfway through so he could rush on to the next, and with his thick Swedish accent, he was difficult for Dad to understand at first. But with great hand-waving and graphic illustrations, and helpful translations by Gust, he made himself fairly clear and always interesting.

In the delicate, obscure way that men have, it finally came out that Kurt had left a good job in Los Angeles as chief mechanic for the Greyhound Bus Lines to come to Nome to look for gold.

"Say, Nordstrom," asked Dad eagerly, "You don't happen to know anything about driving a cat, do you?"

"Well sure, man. Just about everything there is to know. There ain't nothing to it. I drove all kinds of them, from kittys to the real big babies. Down in L.A. for about ten years before I was with Greyhound. I even had my own shop in the garage before we left and I rigged up one of my own cats. Soon as I find a spot that looks good, my wife Helga will come up with the tractor on the next boat. Then I show you just how to do it when we get it up there later this summer."

But of course, Daddy couldn't wait until later. There is no harbor at Nome, so all freight must be put onto barges called lighters, and then towed into the beach. Count Barkavitch had told Gust that the cat-skinner's first job would be to drive the tractor off the lighter and onto the beach.

So, with fancy paper diagrams, much detailed discussion of tractors' whims and tricks, and gesturing and descriptive noises, and Swedish cussing, Kurt coached the cat-skinner how to skin. He even fixed up a dummy operation for Dad to practice on, using the doorknob off the stateroom closet, old shoes, coffee cups, and silverware to simulate the complicated knobs and gadgets of the tractor. The big Swede's English wasn't always too good, but his enthusiasm and patience were endless. And he always assured Daddy, with the confidence of a natural mechanic, that there was really nothing to it . . . simple as driving a car. He'd been doing it for years! But still, Daddy said he couldn't help noticing that there were two fingers missing on one of Kurt's huge hands, and that the thumb was gone on the other.

The sea lost color and the days grew colder as they sailed west and north. The last few days of the trip, only the heartiest passengers made it to the dining room, so Dad and Gust and Kurt ate lavishly. The cat-skinning school went along very well with the doorknobs and cups, but Daddy was more and more nervous as the sea became more choppy and rough.

Count Barkavitch invited the men to his stateroom to discuss the venture, and asked Dad to look over the kitty down in the hold to see that everything was in good order. "The swine from which I purchased the machine was such a miserable fellow. Perhaps you could look it over, sweetheart. Just the expert glance, you know can often detect the flaw."

He served them weak tea and strong whisky, and after several rounds, Big Jack was ready to give an expert opinion on anything. There was no room in the hold for anything but an awkward examination of the machine, but while Gust and the Count watched, Dad tried desperately to figure how Kurt's doorknobs and coffee cups would correspond with the many knobs and bands and wheels and gauges on the panel of the small tractor.

"Everything looks fine, eh little pigeon?" shouted the Count, whacking Daddy on the shoulder.

"Yeah, just swell," he answered weakly. "It all looks very nice." But the Count's enthusiasm wasn't to be dampened by Jack Palmer's sickly look. "Ah, my dears, the Snake River Exploratory Corporation operates only with the finest of equipment, eh boys? I know we will have luck this time. You will soon meet my excellent superintendent, St. George. (Even if he is a bastard of an Englishman.) A few days in Nome to take on provisions and a crew, and then on to the Snake River and the *gold*! . . . Well, Palmer, call on me anytime. It is always a delight to talk to a real *Meister*." And he was gone.

Then, too soon, it was the day and the hour. They arrived in Nome about ten in the morning and the sea was nasty. It was not what you could grace with the word storm, but the waves were slapping and spiteful and splashing in all different directions.

The passengers were taken down a special stairway to the lighter, a clumsy steel barge that took them into the dock at Nome. The harbor was too shallow for the large ship, so all passengers as well as the freight had to be shuttled the last two miles. Dad saw Kurt and Gust get into the last passenger-loaded lighter. The other men looked at them curiously as they shook hands with Daddy grimly and then shouted from the barge below, "Good luck, boy!" The lighter was already bucking and lunging away when Kurt yelled, "Remember, Jack, ignition, spark Number One, compound low, forward gear, low speed. Watch them planks like hell and don't look down!"

Since the tractor had been the last item in the hold, it was the first one out. The men jockeyed the thing into the net and set it gently, gently down onto the bucking barge. "O.K., Palmer, she's all yours!" And for a few minutes, Palmer was the big man. He jumped down onto the lighter and up onto the seat of the tractor—the first time he'd ever been on one in his life. He tried to look casual, but with the plush greatcoat and fur hat it wasn't easy.

"O.K., boys, let's have some blocks under those treads," shouted Dad, over the noise of the sea, trying to sound like he knew what he was doing. All the while, he was repeating to himself the magic words. "Transmission in neutral, choke out, front crank, shift to low, pull back on main clutch." If only he could fit the mess of buttons and knobs and handles in front of him on the panel of the yellow tractor to the instructions Kurt had given him.

He was very high up and very alone as the barge slewed in toward the beach with terrible speed. Then they were there. The men scurried about to secure the barge at the correct distance from the beach, while two of them moved a flimsy-looking plank affair out onto the water. They would just get it maneuvered into position, and then an especially vicious wave would slap it sideways and one corner would tip off into the water.

"Just about got it now, Palmer. You can turn the thing on." Dad turned the front crank and stopped watching the narrow planks. Like a miracle, the tractor shuddered alive. Soon it was puffing and jiggling and roaring as if it knew what it was doing. The man at the ramp jumped back to either side. "O.K. Quick now, before another damn wave slaps 'er over. GO!" He pulled the levers controlling the right and left treads to what he guessed would be a very cautious speed, but the little machine wouldn't respond.

"Go like hell, boy! We ain't got all day," shouted one of the crew.

Dad looked again at the narrow ribbon of planks reaching out over the water to the gray beach and pulled the levers again, hard this time. The cat snorted and shook under him indignantly. The small cleats took hold, and with a head- snapping jolt, it took off straight and fast. He saw the planks come toward him, then they were under him and out of sight, and at last he felt the tractor clutch its tracks into the soft, yielding sand. He looked calm as a king as the cat plowed furiously through the packed sand, past a group of amazed men at the water's edge. Then he saw Kurt Nordstrom running toward him across the beach. Kurt came in at an angle, heading for the right front corner of the tractor. As soon as he was parallel with Dad, still heading straight up from the beach toward the town, he jumped up onto the platform and pulled Daddy's frozen hands from the two sticks, pushing them forward until the machine slowed to a more tractor-like crawl.

"Yumpin' Yesus, boy! What's the hurry? You was aimed off that lighter like a bat out of hell! I never saw such a wild man! Was you trying to bulldoze the town down maybe?"

"It was just like I was hypnotized, Kurt," whispered Dad to his teacher. "If I'd gotten the damn thing in reverse by mistake, I would've been all the way to Russia before I'd ever been able to take my hands off that stick!"

But by this time the crowd on the beach had caught up with them. All were impressed. Nome had never seen a tractor before, but one that flew like a chariot off the lunging old lighter, that was a sight to see! A new hero was born that day.

CHAPTER 9

When Dad roared the little tractor from the lighter to the beach, the whole town watched. Almost everyone always found some good reason to be down at the beach on boat day, except the Eskimos. They didn't need excuses. They just came to frankly stand and stare. They talked quietly among themselves, or, if there were tourists on the boat, they laid out the ivory carvings or fur slippers they had for sale.

It was a very big day in Nome when the first boat came in. The first boat in June brought fresh eggs to people who had been eating eggs that had been in cold storage since September. It brought mining equipment to the men who were living on credit until they got their rigs going and pay dirt showing. The first boat brought in live news of what was going on "outside," for while a few people had radios, the reception was very poor and most of the time only loud static noises came through.

The boat brought back old sourdoughs who'd left the September before on the last boat, meaning to leave Nome forever, to go home and live happily ever after. But usually they found their families strangers, and their friends dead or gone. They found that, after all, there was no place like Nome, and they came back promptly on the first boat. It brought new people to look at and find out about and talk over, and finally absorb. The first boat usually brought in a new crop of teachers too, because the old ones had taught out their year's contract and invariably married some one of the town's many lonely men.

Yes, the first boat was a great thing. People usually began to gather early in the morning, each one wanting to be the first to see the "Old Vic" bringing her cargo of mail, fresh lettuce, real milk, new wives, old wives, and kids grown two inches, supplies and new nurses for the hospital (they always got married too), dress goods for the store, final divorce decrees, and of course, the orders coming from Sears.

So, in a very few minutes Nome knew that the young fella on the tractor was "name of Palmer. Wife and little girl down in Seattle. Gonna work for the Count up to Cripple Creek."

"A real machinist," said the old men sagely. "Ya see the way he whipped that baby off the lighter? Bringin' a thing like that tractor into Nome is going to make a lot of changes around this town. Not much use of panning for gold anymore, I guess. Oh yeah, the Count's back too. Heard him before we could see him, while the lighter was still a long ways out. Calling everybody names, and then handing out the cigars when the crew set him down on the beach. Them Russkies, ain't they a bunch, though? Good to see the old fool back!"

They left the tractor in front of the Hotel, much against Dad's better judgment. "That old dump looks like it's going to cave in right onto the sidewalk. I think we better leave the cat out in the street," he said. But the Count insisted that the Golden Gate Hotel had looked exactly that way for about thirty years, and that the cat was in no immediate danger.

Edgar St. George was waiting in the lobby. The superintendent had been a mining engineer in South America for the past two years, and still had a very dark tan. Although shorts and pith helmet would have suited him better, he was bundled to the ears against the unaccustomed cold. Nome was well into its spring thaw, but the wind off the Bering Sea was still bitter.

After the introductions were made, St. George said, "I've appointed a woman for the cook's position, Count. I believe you're acquainted with her, Gust. It's Mrs. Beck—you know, George Beck's widow. I had a devil of a time finding anyone willing to make the trip up to Cripple Creek, what with things being so, ah . . . uncertain, you know. But the poor woman was glad enough to have the job. They say the old boy didn't leave her much besides the two half-grown youngsters. She seems like a good sport though, and assured me the children are old enough to make the trek."

"Yah, she's a nice strong girl, and I hear she can cook lutfisk just so good as if she was a Swede, instead of a Norske," offered Gust.

The plans were made to leave Nome the following morning. St. George had scrounged around the rusty mining town all that afternoon buying, borrowing, begging, and stealing what they thought they would need to get the Snake River Exploratory Corporation started. Someone had told them that on a certain spot, marked on a very casually drawn map, there was an old dredge, left over from the original gold rush. Several of the old-timers felt that the dredge could be put into working condition by a good mechanic. So St. George, at Dad's suggestion, hired Kurt Nordstrom for the job. Kurt thought the job would probably take only a couple of weeks, and the ground wasn't thawed enough to start his own prospecting yet, anyway. Florence Beck rounded up provisions for the first two weeks and promised to have the food packed and her two children ready to leave at six the next morning.

They found a huge old sled down on the beach in back of the hotel and Kurt mounted it on four wide truck tires. This way they could carry the extra equipment needed to resurrect the dredge and perhaps have room for Florence and her children to ride too. Twenty-seven miles on the tundra is a long walk even for a nice strong girl.

By dinnertime the men felt they had done as much as possible to prepare for the trip, and deserved a little relaxation. St. George, Gust, Kurt, and Dad met the Count in the Blue Fox Saloon to have a friendly drink together, and to discuss the last-minute details of the trip. However, those last-minute details had to remain undiscussed and take care of themselves, because the men soon found themselves in the middle of a raging party—a "Bon Voyage," as the Count would have said.

There was always a good-sized crowd at the Blue Fox. For most of the unattached men in the town, Millie Bergdorf's place or just plain drinking were the only indoor sports available, but the Blue Fox was the real social center of the town. Always, the evening of the first boat's arrival there was sure to be a real whing-ding at the Fox, but the Snake River Exploratory Corporation was something extraordinary. Young men and old began to gather, at first elaborately casual, and then after a couple of drinks, frankly curious and admiring.

The young men were there because they smelled adventure, and they were adventurers, or they wouldn't have been in Nome. The Snake River was one of the first companies to go in to re-mine a creek that had been placer-mined in the old gold rush in 1898. Since the value of the gold ounce went up steadily, and the new machines became practical, it was, all of a sudden, worth-while for a large syndicate to go in and clean up an area that had been mined years before by cruder methods. The Count and St. George had been sent in, along with many other similar small groups, to all parts of Alaska where there was a chance of cleaning up, by a large mining syndicate from Paris. The young men of Nome were excited at the thought that there was money to be made in the hills again.

They only laughed at the old geezers who doddered and dreamed over the old days and the glory that was Nome. But they loved to hear the big-time miners talk. They wanted to hear about bulldozers and cats, draglines and sluices, dredges and Die-sels. And the gold, the gold itself was something that never lost its charm. Just to talk about it, to say the new words, made them feel learned and wise.

While the young men loved to discuss the adventure, it meant life itself again for the old ones. Most of them had come to Nome forty years ago and had worked elbow to elbow with men who'd left the town with millions. They had seen friends, brothers, and partners pick into their little sections of nameless creeks and rivers and find gold that made them rich men in one short summer. "Greasy" Samurian came in to town with only a cotton cook's uniform off the boat and not enough money to pay for his shovel and pan—"They say his kids live in one of them real mansions now in 'Frisco. They had watched "Soapy" Muchison kill his own brother at the long bar in the Golden Gate Hotel for title to the Little M up on Arctic Creek—He went outside that fall and never had to work another day. Lived like a king, they say!"

They had seen the beach, right there at Nome, where the Snake River empties into the sea, when a man staked out his claim for the day by standing in one spot and swinging his #2 shovel around as far as his arms could reach. This circle in the sand was his for that day, and if some fool's head got in the way of the swing of the shovel, too damn bad for him.

"I'm a mind of that summer in ought-four. Ike and I was taking nine, ten hundred dollars a day right off the beach. You remember those days, Barney. Remember how when the sun went down the whole beach looked red, the sand was that full of gold. The red sands of Nome they called it. Why, you'd pick up a pan full of sand and water, slosh it around a couple of times and there she was! An inch deep in the pan, sometimes."

"Yeah Ben, and remember the time Duffy O'Toole pulled out seventeen hundred dollars' worth that Sunday on the beach? And him a good Catholic, too. He got so remorseful for working on the Sabbath, he got drunk up at Belle's place, and he gave her the whole damn sack full . . . seventeen hundred bucks!"

One thing they all agreed on, the good old days were gone forever. But next summer . . . next summer they were going to hit it. The big strike this time. They had secret maps and they had secret codes. They had deathbed instructions and drunken ravings they'd overheard. Or sometimes, as the saying was in Nome, "He just missed too many boats outside." Then they didn't need maps or instructions. They just poked among the litter and garbage on the beach, or took themselves away to the hills to look in peace, alone. They might have to live on squirrels, but they knew they'd find gold . . . maybe tomorrow. . . .

And that night in the Blue Fox Saloon, the fever was fed new fuel. The Count grew more expansive with each drink, and Jack

Palmer spent the profits over and over again in anticipation. St. George became even more clipped and British and told of "how we did it in Rio." The young men were wild to go along to see the tractor move the mountains and streams, and the old ones spouted sage advice. They told where the gold used to be and where it would be again, and how you could tell by the rocks in the creek where the gold would lie.

"Be sure and talk to Snake River Dick when you get there," they said. "He'll be there, all right. He's been working the Snake where it joins Cripple Creek for as long as anyone can remember. Oh, he's a little squirrelly, all right. Only comes into town once or twice a year for salt and sugar and flour, but he can tell you about the Snake. Anything you want to know."

Then they spoke of signs and portents, of the formation of the banks of the streams, of the dead giveaway when there was a little clump of willows after a curve in the stream. And of course, a ptarmigan nest at the creek's edge was always a sure sign of gold.

As the whisky and water poured, the men of Nome drank and talked of gold, and each man wanted to go along. They could see the gold, they could feel it in their hands already, just lying there waiting to be picked up.

CHAPTER 10

At four the next morning "Leaky Pete" and his roommate struck a few blows over whose turn it was to sleep in the armchair, while Jack, Kurt, and Gust wobbled and giggled their way out to the tractor to practice pulling the sled full of equipment. By the time Dad felt completely expert at this maneuver and was ready to celebrate with just one more nightcap, they found the Blue Fox Saloon closed for the night. Their feelings were hurt, but they decided to carry on at the hotel. They would have, too, but somehow they fell asleep instead.

So, two hours later, at 6 A.M., Florence Beck found very little enthusiasm for the adventure that had been so exciting the night before. All the bushiness had gone out of the Count. He looked gray and even his beard sagged and looked frayed at the edges. For once, he didn't say a word; he just shivered a little and sat on one of the food boxes while the men loaded the sled. Even when Dad broke the connecting cable between the sled and the tractor, the Count didn't have the strength to call him *Ti Svolich*, but merely looked more abused and turned his eyes toward the sea.

St. George tried to be brisk, but it was a failure. He had his leggings wrapped too loosely, and they bulged and sagged around his skinny legs. His beret looked droopy instead of jaunty as usual, and he was beginning to lose his temper at the food supplies when they didn't fit properly on the sled. He had Jack and Kurt and Gust move the food and small tools and sleeping bags a dozen ways, but the only result was that several packages of macaroni burst open into the street and one of the sleeping bags came loose. Finally he said, panting a little, "Well, damn it all, boys, we haven't got all day, you know. Just jam the whole bloody mess on and tie it down hard. We've got to be on the way!"

"Yesus, if this little kitty doesn't bust a lung carrying that load, I'm going to write a letter to Caterpillar and tell them they did better than they say in the ads even!" muttered Kurt Nordstrom. "We got the stuff piled on that ark like it was a *Tournahauler*!"

Only Gust was cheerful. The trip into the wilderness with Florence Beck appealed to him tremendously. The more he looked at her, the more protective he felt. "What a shame for a fine young woman like that to be left alone with two half-grown kids," thought Gust. "To have to trek out onto the tundra to cook for a bunch of rough men. Must be terrible for the poor girl; yet how plucky she is through it all. And such a good cook, too."

Florence and the girl and boy were all dressed in hiking pants and boots, heavy wool jackets, and red wool hats, as if they were starting on a gay hunting party. The children chattered excitedly, and continually got in the way of the loading, and held up progress by asking questions. The girl, Minna, laughed a lot, and each time she did, the Count would have to hold his head down firmly so it wouldn't fly off.

At last, all the odd bundles and sacks and awkward tools were on the sled, and the caravan was ready. Gust eased his sleeping bag out from under a heavy case and fluffed it out on top of the loaded sled. "There now, little lady, you and the kids can have a cozy nest for yourselves."

But the gray-faced Count didn't seem to hear him. "Thank you, little dove," he sighed in a trembly voice, as he climbed slowly up to the cozy nest that Gust had prepared for Florence and the children. "I'm really feeling wretched." He lay down and was not heard from again.

Gust was outraged, but Florence said, "Thanks anyway, Gust, but the kids and I don't mind walking. I used to walk miles in the old country. And besides, we got to bed early last night." She winked broadly at Gust and the rest of the men, and they all had to laugh.

The sled had seemed a brilliant idea the night before, but now the great bulky thing, perched high on the truck tires, began to look like the ship that sailed on the land. The tractor and sled clanked through Nome with no good-byes except from the dogs. The Huskies were furious at the strange noises of the cat, and at each street they set up a howling barrage as the Snake River Exploratory Corporation passed by.

They were soon out of sight of Nome and into the tundra, following the Snake River toward the hills. Walking twenty-seven miles anywhere is a good day's work, but the tundra is something special. It grows in spongy, grass-matted hillocks, just far enough apart so you cannot step from one hump to another, yet just close enough together so you can't walk between them. By June the earth was thawed to about six inches and the sun melted the tundra so that each step was a project. Look to see how far the next hump is . . . pull your foot out of the muck of the last step . . . next step into the muck again . . . then start over again. The cat did very well on the lumpy terrain, but walking on it was a chore. Soon everyone was exhausted, as their hiking boots became heavy and heavier with mud.

By nine o'clock it was very warm and the party stopped on a little rise to shed their jackets and hats. From the slight hill, they could look back over the flat country. Nome was still disappointingly close.

"Looks to me as if we've only covered about five miles," said St. George. "But then, if the desert can make a man see a mirage, this tundra could drive you mad."

"The wild flowers are real pretty though," offered Minna, and the young boy was still frisky enough to pick a bouquet of wild iris for his mother. He even stuck one delicate blossom behind his ear. Everyone took off a layer of woolen sweaters and jackets, and the sweet wind off the sea dried the sweat on their arms and faces. Florence brought a large thermos of hot coffee out of a box that was, amazingly enough, accessible and easy to open. There were sugar lumps packed close by that the children enjoyed, and Florence and Gust and Kurt used them for *Klumpsukkerr*, in the

Swedish way. They folded them into their lower lips and sucked the coffee through it like three Buddhas.

The warm sunshine, exercise, and hot coffee improved all the hangovers except the Count's. He hadn't moved since he'd crawled to the nest on top of the sleeping bags. When Florence offered him coffee, he only moaned and turned his head the other way. So St. George rolled him over a little more and searched his pants pockets for the map. "Ah, here we are, ladies and gentlemen. I think we've got about five miles still to go following the Snake before we strike out cross-country. I thought surely we'd make better time than this. We'll have to speed it up a bit or we'll never make Cripple Creek by tonight."

By this time the group had been sitting still long enough so the shy creatures of the tundra began to show themselves. There were hundreds of tiny ground squirrels poking curious heads out of their holes in the tundra, and they saw a huge swarm of the pheasant-like ptarmigan flying just across the river. In every direction the tundra rolled endlessly away like an ocean, with not a single tree to break the horizon. A few puny willows were growing there, but they were only two or three feet high because of the severe winters. But the wild flowers covered the ground for miles. There were carpets of pale dwarf iris pierced through with vivid spikes of royal blue lupin. Wild honeysuckle of a creamy yellow shade intertwined almost every hillock of tundra.

As the party started forward again, they all felt better, and the tractor left a wake of perfume from the crushed flowers in its path. St. George whistled "John Peel," Gust and Florence chatted cozily in a special combination of Swedish and Norwegian, the children played guessing games about the objects they passed, and, as they humped along over the tundra, Jack and Kurt dreamed of the gold they would find. Only the Count was still wrapped in the remains of the night before.

Shortly before ten thirty they started off cross-country from the Snake River. "The old boy who gave me the map said the Snake takes a great meander here, and if we take off due east for about ten miles as the crow flies, we'll come right back to the river and save ourselves about fifteen miles. So, due east it is, eh boys?" St. George was feeling very much the explorer by now and continued, "We can probably make camp by the river for lunch."

By three that afternoon they were still traveling due east with not a sign of the Snake River. Florence was frantic with Per who kept sitting down to rest. "Go ahead, Mamma," he would call. "Just go ahead and I'll run to catch up in a minute." The three men were weary and griping at each other, but Florence and Minna trudged on like soldiers. By this time the Count had come to life and was directing from the top of the loaded sled.

"Listen to me, English boob! You must have taken the wrong trail while I was unconscious. You've led this innocent party into the wilds of Alaska—into the very jaws of monsters, doubtless! Sweet God! Why must I surround myself with such feeble incompetents?"

"Now I say, Count. While you were sleeping it off, I followed that damn map exactly. It's the fool map that is at fault. That's what happens when you take the word of some crazy old miner, and I'm going to see that the Syndicate hears about it when . . . ."

Then Florence Beck interrupted softly but firmly. "All right now, boys. We are going to eat. We've climbed over two mountains since you said we'd stop for lunch. Jack, stop the machine. We eat now. No more arguments about who did what. We must go until we find the river again, but we can't go any further without a little stuffing in us. Please to climb down, Mr. Count."

Florence and Minna unpacked boxes while Jack and Gust made a fire in the small stove. Soon she had several cans of beans simmering around plump wieners. A cool potato salad and thick slabs of homemade bread appeared, and they finished with coconut cake and more coffee. The meal worked like a miracle. The Count and St. George stopped fighting, Jack took Per up on his lap to help drive, and the Count insisted on the two ladies riding with him in the sled. Gust was even more impressed with Florence's cooking, and the party went on with new hope.

As soon as they reached the next little rise, they saw the Snake River lying below them, like a perfect replica of the map. "There now, my dears," shouted the Count triumphantly, as if he had personally planted the river there, "didn't I tell you I would lead you to the right place? I have an instinct about these things!"

"Well, now that you have saved us all from the jaws of those monsters, old boy, what say we all hip it along a little faster," sneered the Englishman. "If we're to make Cripple Creek by tonight, we'll really have to dash. We're away behind schedule."

"Of course, my heart's delight. Hop along as fast as you like. However, I am an old man and am entitled to a few of the comforts." With that, he climbed up by Minna, put his head in Florence's lap, and lit up a cigar.

The course they took that first time into Cripple Creek looked as if it had been plotted by a local drunkard with a mean streak. They crossed and re-crossed landmarks, so they knew they must have made several complete circles. They went over two mountains that could easily have been skirted if they'd known the trail. They stopped for a hurried dinner at a place on the river that they found afterward was called Mosquito Junction, where they were almost devoured by the huge insects.

Finally, at 9 P.M., Florence Beck again called a halt to the stumbling men. "All right, boys, this is it. We aren't going any further tonight. The kids and me are O.K. We have ridden since lunchtime, but Kurt and Gust and Mr. St. George are like ghosts, so pale they are. The gold will wait another day yet, I think." Florence seemed to have taken over as the mother of the lost boys, and the Count was too tired to object.

"O.K., Florence," said Dad. "You start unpacking the sleeping bags, and Gust and Kurt and I will follow the river up to the next hill and see if we can spot a sheltered place for the tent."

Even at nine in the evening, the sun still lighted the tundra, but the wind was ice-cold from the sea. They unhooked the sled, with the Count still on top blowing cigar smoke and bad advice to everyone, while Jack drove the little cat to the top of the rise.

"Hey!" shouted Dad back to the others, "I think I see the dredge! Right down there!"

"What do you mean, young fool?" hollered the Count, running uphill toward the cat. "You think you see the dredge!

Do you see it? Do you not see it? Da or Nyet, which is it?" He puffed up the hill.

"Well sir, it seems to be kind of, well . . . ah, sunk. See, right down there where the two streams come together." The men looked down on the wreck of an ancient dredge on a water-logged wooden barge, half sunken into the silt of the river. There was a little shack on one corner of it, still above water, covered almost completely with wild honeysuckle vines.

"Ah, let me feast my eyes on our lovely location," drooled the Count. "Beautiful . . . *krasavitza*! We have only to pump out a little water, and it will be a lovely dredge. That foul St. George is a good engineer, no matter what a beast he has been on the trail. The gold he'll have pouring through our fingers in no time! Kurt, you go back and tell the others we have arrived at our destination. We'll ride down and take a closer look, my little pigeon."

As they rumbled down toward the dredge, they could see evidence of what looked like fresh digging all along the river bank. The Count pointed to the turned-up earth, saying, "Is it not amazing how the intense cold preserves? It's as if these holes were dug yesterday, instead of maybe thirty years ago." As they pulled in close to the dredge Jack said, "I don't know about that, Count. Unless the cold preserved those little flowers too, there's something funny around here." He pointed to a neat row of dwarf marigolds blooming in a dozen tin cans, set along the edge of the little shack on the dredge. Just then, directly in front of them, an old white- haired man hopped out of the shack, picked up a large piece of angle iron and ran across the dredge and onto the path. He was dressed in high fur mukluks (native shoes) and very dirty white underwear. He brushed his curls out of his eyes with one hand, but still held the angle iron firmly.

"Howdy, boys. I heard you was comin' out this way. I'm Snake River Dick."

"Ah yes, Mr. Dick. They told us in town you might be able to help us. I am Count Barkavitch of the Snake River Exploratory Corporation. We've come to raise the dredge, and I . . . ."

"Not this dredge, you ain't! This is my dredge! I been here on the creek since 1900, and no old fossil like you is goin' to march in and take her away from me. I got the claim filed right in to Nome, so you can take your fool machine and go right back to where you came from!"

"Did you hear that?" screamed the Count, standing up on top of the cat. "He called me old fossil! Boy, run over him! Drive the machine right over the crazy old man. Out of the way, old *Durak*, or I have my man grind you into the earth you stand on!"

But Snake River Dick only planted his mukluks farther apart in the trail, grasped his iron club more firmly, and laughed up at the Count. "Come ahead, you damn furriner *fossil*. I'm ready!"

The Count glared down at the old man until his eyes bulged and his face was purple. "Bah, you pig you. If this were Russia, I'd flatten you like a fly! Drive ahead, Palmer!"

"Come on, Count," said Dad softly. "We'll spend the night at the tent, and we'll talk to Dick again in the morning." As he turned the tractor around in the narrow trail, the old miner spat a great splatter of snoose on the retreating tracks, and hobbled back to his dredge.

"Listen mister," Jack said then to the Count, "I agreed to any odd jobs that needed doing on this deal, but that sure doesn't include running over old men with tractors. I've had about enough of . . . ."

"Now now, brother, we mustn't be hasty. You're perfectly right about the old fellow. He's obviously insane. Maybe been eating squirrel out here by himself a few years too many. But violence would be awkward. I'm sure there is some legal settlement I can arrange."

When they got back to the others, Gust had the tent up and Florence was dishing up the last of the coconut cake and fresh coffee.

"Well, my children, I've located the dredge, and as soon as we've disposed of this mad old fellow of a Snake River Dick we can go full tilt at the gold." As the men ate, the Count explained to St. George, "You see, the old man has some crazy idea that he has legal claim to the dredge. Obviously absurd, of course, but there is the complication of a claim filed in the town."

When the Count finished his cake, he insulted Florence terribly by insisting on brewing his own tea. As he sipped the hot drink gently, he sprang up suddenly. "I have the solution! St. George, you—no, you Palmer—you are the United States citizen. Tomorrow you go into Nome. You file a complaint at the Federal Courthouse that this Dick person is insane, unable to competently manage a valuable property. The police cart the old fellow off, and we take over the dredge! Beautiful, what? And I can . . . ."

"You can forget my part in your plan, Barkavitch. After three days with this sweet little outfit, I'm not so sure just who's crazy around here. But I'm not going to send the old guy to the nut house for you! Now if you still want me to go into Nome in the morning, I'll walk in, but I won't be back!"

The Count spat a great mouthful of tea on the ground and threw the tin cup after it. "Dear Sweet Heaven! Am I surrounded by imbeciles here in this barbaric land? This is a matter of gold—not the insignificance of one old man who should have died years ago anyway. Why, he'd be as happy as a singing bird in some cozy asylum. Come, St. George, tell this idealistic boy how things of this sort are managed in the mining business."

"Well now, Count, I'm inclined to think we could get rid of the old nuisance easily by offering him a small sum. Probably be tickled to get into Nome and blow it up to his cronies and all, you know. Few hundred ought to do it, eh?"

"Jesus, you see how I am plotted against by a group of *boys?* Conspired against, humiliated by greenhorns? Very well, I know nothing, then. I am the slave, the trash-carrier. We shall have the two Swedish peasant children conduct all matters of delicacy and diplomacy from this day on. Possibly Mrs. Beck will act as Chairman of the Board, and the young Engineer of the Tractor will sit on his machine and direct us where to put in our shovels for the gold!"

He stomped into the tent and yanked out his sleeping bag. "High Heaven! I'd just as soon sleep with a pack of . . . *of nuns!* He strode away from the fire about fifty feet, threw down his sleeping bag, and zipped himself into it furiously, boots and all, with only his beard bristling out at the top.

Minna and her brother started to giggle and only a stem eye from Florence and a cookie stuffed in the mouths prevented hysteria. The men ate cookies, too, and drank another cup of coffee, and tried to look solemn, but only succeeded in looking sheepish instead. Although the sun still showed late afternoon, the warmth was gone and the tent shielded their sleeping bags from a damp wind off the Bering Sea.

Florence waited until the exhausted men and children were asleep. Even watchful Gust was snoring, so she walked softly out to the Count. "Come, Count Barkavitch. It would do none of us any good if the leader of this expedition was to get sick. This damp night air is terrible for a man's lungs!"

CHAPTER 11

A s it turned out, Snake River Dick got five thousand dollars for his claim and the dredge on Cripple Creek. After the old miner gave long and detailed instructions as to just where the gold was and how to get the dredge working, Dad drove him into Nome. They made a triumphant entrance, directly to the swinging doors of the Blue Fox Saloon, where Dick insisted on treating Dad in return for saving his mine and his life.

"I know'd you wouldn't run over me with that thing!" he cackled. "Yessir boys, that old varmint of a Rooshin was goin' to squash me right into the tundra like a gopher, but this kid here tells him what's what. Hee . . . yeah, I knowed when I saw your eye, you wasn't goin' to run down old Snake River Dick!"

When Daddy left the Blue Fox, he said it looked doubtful that the $5,000 would last out the night, but apparently it did as Dick left on the next boat for "outside" to stay with a daughter in Seattle.

Meanwhile, the Snake River Exploratory Corporation camp was having a good summer. The days were warm and sunny and lasted almost all night, so St. George and the rest of the men worked ten to twelve hours every day. But they still had time to have fun, too.

Dad had been hunting since he was a boy, so besides cat-driving and building a permanent camp house, he was the game-keeper. It was against the law for white men to kill reindeer, so they called them "caribou" instead, and shot one every two weeks or so. The reindeer ate only willow shoots and berries, so the meat of the young animals had a delicate flavor and was very tender. Gust specialized in crusty caribou steak broiled over an open fire, while Florence became an expert at caribou pie under a flaky crust, or caribou stew with tiny dumplings floating on top. Another fresh meat that supplemented their meals was ptarmigan. These grouse-like birds flew over the tundra in flocks of thousands, and were so tame that Daddy said he was almost ashamed to shoot them. When you shot at one of the flock while they were feeding, the rest flustered up into the air and then settled back down ten feet away like pigeons in front of City Hall. They fed so exclusively on the wild blueberries during the summer that they actually had a delicious faint blueberry flavor, and the meat was slightly purple in color during the season.

Florence and Minna and Per picked pails of the berries for pies and muffins and blueberry pancakes. Each berry was huge, about the size of a tame raspberry. They were a dusty purple-mauve on the outside, but clear and translucent inside, with none of the mushy texture of the blueberries sold in stores. They grew so thick on the small bushes on the tundra that Minna and Per could pick a regular garden bucketful in about fifteen minutes. Florence didn't even add any flour or other thickening to the berries for pies; just a generous cupful of sugar and the natural juice of the berries made a perfect syrup.

Dad found an old ice-cream freezer in Nome for Florence, so wild blueberry ice cream became one of the favorites of the camp. There was seldom any left over after the hard-working men had finished, but when Florence made enough to last till Sunday, she merely had Gust dig a hole in the tundra about a foot and a half deep, and there it was—a perfect deep freezer.

It was a fine summer for all the men, but Gust was in heaven. He was in love, as innocently and naively in love as a twenty-year-old. The fact that Florence Beck had been a wife and mother for fifteen years and had managed her family like a good top sergeant didn't stop Gust. He treated her like the village belle. He always took her arm carefully over the mud holes and piles of dirt stacked here and there in the camp, and frowned ferociously at the Count whenever he swore in front of his darling. And he fretted constantly over the rugged conditions under which his "little Flicka" (an easy 185 pounds) had to live and work.

As for Florence, she was a little embarrassed by the whole affair, but still very pleased. When Gust and Jack finished building the permanent camp, Gust insisted on a separate room being added for Florence. She assured St. George that such luxury was unnecessary, and that she had signed on knowing all about the rough conditions in mining camps. However, since the Count had moved into Nome at the beginning of the month, the men decided that the Snake River Exploratory Corporation could well afford this nicety for the only woman in a thousand miles who could make wild blueberry sourdough pancakes.

"Besides," offered Gust, "just think what those old klakkers in to Nome would be saying about such a fine young woman sleeping right in the same tent with a pack of rough men."

So, by the middle of July, Florence had her private room and everyone was happy, especially Gust. He even made a special trip into town with Dad to buy the paint. Copenhagen blue it was, with pink trim.

And along with the building of the permanent camp, the men had pumped the water out of the old barge and raised the fallen dredge to busy respectability. Kurt Nordstrom turned out to be a genius with the temperamental old machinery, and was soon in charge of all operations on the dredge. The tractor was put to work to push great mounds of dirt into the river where it was washed and refined for the gold. Then the "stacker" would haul it all out again and throw it up in mountainous tailing piles. This left Gust to the general labor and clean-up work around the camp, while Jack Palmer had plenty of time to become an excellent cat-skinner. He made one or two trips into Nome each week for supplies and equipment as they needed them, and between trips he was the "caribou" hunter and carpenter foreman.

It was also about this time that Florence got the biggest cook stove in the Territory of Alaska. It was one of three formerly used in the Golden Gate Hotel, a relic on Front Street, that had had its heyday during the gold rush about 1900. Dad had gone to town on one of his foraging trips for food supplies, and happened to ask where he might buy a second-hand stove for the camp. Mrs. Wagner at the store told him that she didn't know of any for sale around town and that a new one would probably have to be ordered from "outside."

"But say, Jack, the thing to do, if your cook isn't too fussy about what she gets, is to go down on Front Street where all the old deserted miners' shacks are. Most of the old coots have died, or if they pulled out, they just left things the way they were. Most everything's gone but the brass beds and the stoves. You could probably take your pick of the lot."

So Dad took her advice and drove the cat down to the oldest section of Nome where Front Street ran for about a mile along the ocean. The Imperial Hotel and all the shacks near it had burned during the winter of 1920, but between the burn and the more modern stores and buildings were the skeletons of the gold rush. The dark gray houses and spindly saloons rattled and whispered together in the wind, and nobody knew why they didn't blow into the sea. Each year they grew scalier and scabbier as if they were preserved in the ocean salt and held up as a reminder of what greed leaves behind.

As one miner moved out of his one- or two-room lean-to another would soon be around to take out the doors and windows to use in his own shack, so it was easy to see how the fire had razed whole blocks at a time. The windowless buildings made perfect tinder, and the openings allowed the fire to leap easily from one to the next. Sometimes an Eskimo family would move into one for a winter quarters, or a stray dog would take a few years' lease. Lena Ikiyuna and her nine half-Eskimo kids lived in one that was too dirty even for the dogs. But for the most part, the buildings were empty except for the rats. It was hot that summer and the new baby rats were fat and healthy already. The shacks stank from them, worse than skunk.

Jack finally decided on a little four-burner, pot-bellied affair in a one-room cabin next to the old Golden Gate Hotel. It was badly rusted and one of the round lids was missing, but he figured Gust could rig up something to fix it. However, even the smallest iron stove is a heavy load for one man, so he called next door to the thin, gray-haired old Negro man who sat on the stoop of the huge empty hotel. Joe Easiola was his name, and he always insisted he was Ethiopian, not Negro.

"Why sure, Mr. Palmer. I be glad to assist you out to the tractor with the cook stove, but I seem to recollect we got a couple extra stoves right here to the hotel that's in better shape than that thing you got there. Step inside while I hunt 'em up."

The vague-eyed old man led Dad through the cool, high-ceilinged lobby, past the semicircular mahogany main desk. He pushed through lovely louvered doors to the enormous dining hall fronting on the ocean.

"Right through the salon, here. This used to be the kitchen in the good times, but now Maxwell and me stay here altogether. Only room without the windows bust out." The black old man picked his way carefully through stacks of boxes, piles of old newspapers, and a skinny dog nursing a litter of puppies, to the shelves at the end of the room. He gently poked an old fur parka, wedged in between hundreds of *National Geographics* stacked on the shelves.

"Rise up, boy, and help me find them old cook stoves we got around here." A beautiful little boy of about seven rolled out of the molting fur. He was slightly darker than an Eskimo, and had large soft curls ringed around his head.

"This is my boy, Mr. Palmer—Maxwell Selassie Easiola. Mr. Palmer here's the tractor-driver fellow, honey. And I said he could use one of those old stoves we got around here somewheres. You recollect where that big old six-burner thing is, child?"

The boy's velvet eyes were still full of sleep, but he was cheerful and alert. "Why sure, Papa, you remember, we moved both those old cook stoves into the bridal suite when you was married with Lena Ikiyuna. I'll find Slim and Nick to help us move it out, if they're at home." The little fellow hauled on a pair of pants and some mukluks and went to find the men.

"That's a fine-looking boy you have there, Joe. Seems bright as a button, too," said Dad to the old man.

"Yes sir, he's a good boy. Helps out here at the hotel a lot. But he's goin' on about eight this summer sometime, I think. I got to think about getting that Maxwell some schooling. I figure I might have a little trouble with the school ladies. His mother was an Eskimo, you see, and I sure wouldn't want him to have to go way up to the Eskimo school. But come on into the bridal suite here, sir. We'll see can't we find that old stove for you."

They entered a long narrow room off the kitchen, which also fronted on the Bering Sea. There were two long graceful windows opening onto a balcony, long since sucked into the ocean, and under each window was placed an enormous iron cooking stove. In the huge room, they looked like two dainty dressing tables. The narrow panes of the windows had been patched with different pieces of boards and packing boxes, old calendar covers, and tatters of canvas. The different colors and textures made them look like stained-glass windows in a church. Centered between the two windows was an intricately carved black teakwood grand piano with most of its keys missing, and the white coverings of the remaining keys flapping up like old shoe soles.

The walls and window drapings had once been done in heavy burgundy plush velvet, patterned with gold roses, but now the lovely material had been frozen and thawed until it hung in molding strips from the ceiling to the floor. The elaborate brass headboard stood eight feet tall on the opposite wall, like a pipe organ, and the bed could have been the altar, swathed in the same gloomy red velvet hangings. But some of Queenie's puppies had claimed it for their own and dragged the draperies down for a warm nest in the middle of the bed. A gilded candle holder hung on crazily by one last nail above the bed, while its mate had given up and rolled under the piano with some empty beer bottles.

"Take your pick of the stoves, Mr. Palmer. I think Maxwell's got Swenson and Slim to help tote. Try not to mind the smell of that Swenson. He's the one who drives the honey wagon, and in the summer you can hardly stand to be in the same room with him. But he's very strong . . . We're in here, boys.

"Say Palmer, that was sure as hell something the way you whing-dinged that tractor off the lighter!" said Slim. "I told my partner, 'Now there's a kid who knows how to handle machinery!" How are things going out at the place there? Barkavitch was blabbering away about how much gold you're going to haul out of Cripple Creek, but he's such a gasser. We got a few hundred bucks put by and we were thinking . . . ."

"Never mind that now, gentlemen. You just truck this old stove out so's Mr. Palmer can get on his way, and when you're through, Maxwell and I'll have some hot coffee waitin' for you in the kitchen," commanded Joe Easiola, motioning Swenson and Slim over to the stove.

"O.K., Joe," yelled Swenson. "You rustle up some caviar and champagne and we'll all have high tea in the *Salon*! . . . Poor old coot is crazy as a bedbug. Thinks this old dump is still a goin' concern." The large man heaved one shoulder up against the nearest stove and it started to move. Jack and Slim scrambled to the other side and had to step lively not to have their toes flattened by the stove, as the giant man shoved it over the creaking, sagging floors.

"You boys run on ahead and open the doors and get things out the way." The two other men scampered ahead, opened the main front door, and before Dad could even give directions, Big Swenson had the stove dumped on its side on the trailer in back of the cat.

Slim, Swenson, and Dad went back through the dim hotel lobby and into the kitchen. The sun was shining on the ocean and threw wiggling reflections into the room, lighting the highest corners. The little boy had set out odd cups and saucers, sugar and a tin of canned milk at the far end of a long, narrow table. It had been an inlaid-fruitwood dining table in its day, French Rococo in style, richly carved, each of the many leaves made to fit perfectly. But since then it had been used for a chopping board, fish-cleaning area, and general catch-all. With all its leaves, it stretched about thirty feet across the length of the kitchen, and Joe Easiola had it piled four feet high with thirty years' collection of junk. Whenever he or one of his Eskimo women was through with a meal or a stack of funny papers, they would shove the debris to the end of the table and start fresh.

On the table there were dirty pots and dog dishes, worn-out parkas, snow shoes, and a bicycle with a wheel gone, four purple velvet Napoleon hats with "I.O.O.F." written on in gold (Independent Order of the Odd Fellows), a busty dress form, ancient San Francisco newspapers and *Godey's Ladies Books*, two or three dishpans crusted thick with ancient pancake dough, old food cases and empty whisky bottles, cracked lamp chimneys, and Eskimo ivory carvings. Scattered through the whole mess were the remains of a set of fine Haviland china that must have once served fifty people. Through a dusty overlay of dried-on food, an ornate gold design could be traced on melon-pink plates, soup bowls, cups and saucers, salad plates, tiny butter dishes, and even little salt dishes. There was only about six feet of clear space left on the beautiful, battered table, and Joe seated the three men there, carefully pushing in their orange boxes as they sat down.

"Hey, Old Joe," said Swenson, "You only got six feet left on this thing. What you going to do when this junk crowds you right off the end?"

"Well, Mr. Swenson, I figure this table and me will be finished right about together. That'll be just about right, too, since we both come together to the Golden Gate. Mr. LaFavor, that was the boss then, he ordered a Class A, Number One table to serve fifty people and a Class A, Number One boy to wait. And that was me. Yes, sir, this table was a pretty thing in the years gone by, Mr. Palmer, especially when all the pretty ladies were sittin' around it, laughing and nodding like flowers in their pink satin dresses. I remember when LaFavor brought the 'Frisco Beauty Belles up to Nome. It was a pretty rough bunch we had here then, but they were all real nice ladies, and I used to play that big piano while they sang. That was before I got the rheumatism. Anyway,

I'd play and they'd sing, and one time when Aurora Rose and LaFavor's wife got in a hassle over . . . ."

"Come off it, Joe," said Slim. "Palmer doesn't want to listen to your old pipe dreams. He's digging for real gold now, and we want to hear about it. What about the old dredge, Jack? How much are you takin' out a day now?"

The old man was undisturbed by the rude Swede. He poured another cup of coffee for the men and pulled Maxwell and one of Queenie's puppies onto his lap.

No, I'd really like to hear about the old days, Joe. I guess you must have been around here when this town was something to see. But Florence and the boys will be waiting for me, so I'd better start back. I'll come again when we can talk. Come on, Maxwell. I'll take you for a ride on the tractor as far as the Imperial and back. . . . Thanks a lot for the stove, Joe. And you too, Slim and Swenson, for the help. I know our cook will really appreciate this thing. You'll all have to take a trip out to the camp for wild blueberry pie someday."

CHAPTER 12

So that was how Florence got her stove. But of course, Mama and I never knew about any of these interesting times until Daddy told us about them many months later. Although this would have been the ideal occasion for those chatty, informative letters that people preserve for the family Bible, Daddy wrote exactly four times that summer.

The first note, when he arrived, said:

> Dear Alice, Arrived safe. Will write soon, Love, Jack.

The second one, about the end of July, was the one that had her worried. It said:

> Dear Alice, Don't worry. I'm feeling fine. Hope you are the same. Love, Jack.

Coming from Daddy, this was too much. The first letter was an absolute necessity to let her know that his money had lasted, that he hadn't starved on the boat, that he had learned to drive the tractor, and that he hadn't fallen overboard.

"But that second one," said Mama, "That was just giddy extravagance, coming from Jack. A long letter like that for nothing! I simply couldn't figure it out. At first I wondered if he had lost his job, but then Grama and I finally decided that he was probably just lonely, had plenty of time on his hands, and that all was well."

It was later that week that Mama saw Gust's sister, Mrs. Erickson, downtown. She had taken Gust's dog, Shorty, and the pups, when Mama went to work, so of course, the two women had to have a long talk about the mother and children, about the lovely homes she's found for the girl pups, and how Shorty looked when she saw the snapshots of Gust in a parka at Nome. They had a good chat over a cup of coffee, but just as they got up to leave, Mrs. Erickson took Mama's hand and patted it.

"Oh, and Mrs. Palmer, I was so glad to hear about Jack doing so well. Gust wrote that his leg is going to be *all right*!" she said.

"What leg?" Mama squawked, over the genteel buzz of the tearoom, grabbing her back to the table. "What about Jack's leg?"

Poor Mrs. Erickson looked like she was going to cry. "Why, his leg that he chopped with the axe! But if I had any idea that you didn't know about it, I wouldn't have said a word to upset you. But it's nothing to worry about, dear. They say it's a wonderful little hospital, and now that the danger of gangrene is past, everything is fine and . . . ."

"Hospital, gangrene . . ." she whispered. "I think I'd better sit down."

Mrs. Erickson was so embarrassed and flustered at having let such a bad-looking cat out of the bag that she could hardly speak, but she managed to give Mama as much of the story as she knew from Gust's letters.

"Well, I guess he was chopping on this here big timber on the shovel affair, the dredge. And the axe blade flew off and cut his leg. Not so bad though, Alice. So they took him right into town to the hospital. Not so bad, at all, really. There was the infection, is all . . . Oh, you're pale, child. I just wouldn't have been the one to tell you for the world."

"No, no, I'm fine. Just tell me."

"Well, Gust said it was pretty bad for a while, but you know how men are, such babies. There wasn't any gangrene, and they didn't have to cut his leg off, and like I said, the lovely little hospital and all, and the nurses take such good care—oh, not too good, but just like nice nurses, you know."

"I don't know what to think. There's so much I should know about. Maybe I should be there with him," moaned Mama.

"Well now, dear, I've got all Gust's letters saved at home and I'll have Sven drive out to your place with them tonight. Now I've really got to get home, but *don't worry!* Not a thing to worry about!"

And as it all turned out, Mrs. Erickson was right. No permanent damage was done to Daddy's leg, and he was out of Nome General Hospital by the first of August. He favored his left leg slightly for many months afterward, but he was able to drive the tractor again, and was soon Florence Beck's favorite project at the camp.

"I tell you, Jack," she insisted, "it's that hospital and their fancy nurses that make you look like a patsy, standing there so thin. Shame for them that they feed a man on thin mush and bone soups, when what he needs is lots of butter on the pancakes and meat and potatoes to stick to the ribs. Don't think you can walk out of any camp of mine looking like a skeleton at the end of the summer! What would they say in to Nome if I let you go looking hungry like this? After this you eat three squares, let the sun shine down on that bad leg on Sundays, and Gust says he will shoot the reindeer and ptarmigan until we break camp."

St. George even insisted that Count Barkavitch pay the hospital bill. This was quite a concession, because although the men of the Snake River Exploratory Corporation were having a wonderful time, they weren't finding the gold. The Count made several trips out to the camp to rave about Americans who chop their legs all for a few weeks of soft living in a hospital, about greenhorn Swedes who can't even speak the language, and especially about the stupidity of the English.

"I tell you, St. George, the gold is here, under our very noses. I personally can smell it. You are wasting the precious summer looking in the wrong places. You are not thorough. You are taking advices of fools and idiots and silly engineering formulas, instead of from me! Me, who once worked at the right hand of the *Czar!*

I'm coming all the way across that vile tundra, tearing myself away from important goings-on in the town, to tell you where to dig. Now take that lovely little Nordstrom by his ear and tell him to dig right in this spot here where I'm pointing my finger. *Da*— right here! I assure you, this is the gold vein, and if you are all too stupid to find it, I wash my hands of all of you. I shall write the Syndicate, and you will all be replaced by a band of blind, grunting Neanderthals, who at least will know how to follow my excellent orders I give!"

And so, because they had dug everywhere else, St. George did try the area that the Count had indicated. After about a week of dredging, they found a rich vein of gold, heading off away from the creek.

"By God, old Barkavitch will never let us forget this, boys," shouted St. George happily. "But we've really got to move now. There's already a bit of a nip to the air, and they say the first snow usually falls about the end of the month."

As the dredge gouged more and more loads of tundra away, the gold vein seemed to widen and become even richer. Gust, Jack, Kurt, and St. George all worked twelve to fourteen hours a day, as the earth poured into the sluice boxes, and the tiny nuggets became larger and more numerous.

"Gee, it's beautiful stuff, ain't it, Jack?" said Gust softly. "I just like to hold it in my hand, it feels so nice and heavy. Such a pretty ring a few of these nuggets would make, eh?"

"Yeah, I know what you mean, Gust. I like to hold it, too. But I don't think of a gold ring. I think of nice green paper dollars, and how it's going to feel to say to that boob of a credit manager down at Ernst Hardware, 'Here's your money, every last cent of it!' And Builders Brick and Fuller Paint, and Graystone Sand and Gravel and the whole damn bunch of them."

In the meantime, Builders Brick and Ernst Hardware and all the rest of the creditors still sent their polite letters every month and made their embarrassed phone calls every week. Actually, Mama said they were as good about the money as they could be. She talked to the young fellow from the credit department at Elliott Bay Lumber so often that they became quite good friends.

"I hate to call so often, Mrs. Palmer. I know you're doing your best, and I want you to know you're not alone in this mess. Why, we've got lots of accounts that were just like yours; perfect credit for twenty years and then all of a sudden—whamo! Just haven't got the money to pay. It's still my job to call though, so you'll be hearing from us. Say hello to your mother for me."

However, Mama was making $18.50 per week at the grocery store by then, so we were living quite well, compared to many others. Grama had a large garden going in the back yard, and twenty chickens in the barn. The garden looked like Mrs. Wiggs's cabbage patch, but it did have beautiful new peas, slender crisp beans, and corn that popped with sweet juice when you bit into it. Grama was never one to regiment or organize anything, so her garden looked nothing like the neat plots pictured in the seed catalogues. She'd sow a handful of corn here and there, with a pumpkin seed mixed in, because "a nice Jack-O-Lantern looks so kinda spooky in among the corn husks for the children at Halla-Eve, you know." And if a sunflower started up among the lettuce, Grama would never think of weeding it out. She called them Volunteers, and "they all want to live," she'd say. "Besides, the youngsters love to eat the salted sunflower seeds."

The neighbors fertilized and sprinkled and sprayed, but usually ended up asking Grama what on earth she did to get such beautiful vegetables. But she was always as vague as a good cook about the whole thing. "Oh, just give 'em plenty of water, and remember to thank God for the sunshine."

We ate lots of chicken that summer, too. Mama's brother, Uncle Max, would come out to do the execution, and everyone enjoyed Sunday chicken dinner except Grama. She said she knew every chicken as a friend and missed each one when it was gone. By the end of August we'd eaten all the young hens except Gram's two pets. The old hen had trampled these two when they were baby chicks, and had broken a leg of each of them. Gram had carefully splinted them with matchsticks and twine, but she insisted they still were "clubfoots." "Why, it wouldn't be decent to eat the poor cripples!"

One evening, late in the summer, Grama had been out in the barn to tuck in her two clubfooted hens. "They probably feel strange with so many of the others gone," she said. And just as she lifted the last hen onto the nest, it laid an egg in Grama's hand! She flew out of the barn, carefully holding the warm egg. "Alice, come and look! If that don't beat all!"

Then, just as Mama looked out the back window to see what was going on, Grama's feet slipped out from under her and she fell heavily onto one of the concrete steppingstones. Mama ran out to where she lay and she still had the egg in her hand, still unbroken.

"I think I'm hurt pretty bad, Alice," Grama said in a small apologetic voice. "I can't move my leg."

By the time the doctor arrived, Uncle Max was there too, and he and Mama carried Gram into the house. Dr. Kintner gave her a shot of morphine and a strong sedative to sleep the night through, and by morning he telephoned. "I'm afraid your mother is going to have to spend quite a few months in the hospital, Alice. Sara is almost seventy years old now and a hip fracture at her age is no joke. The ambulance is on the way now, and I'll call you again as soon as we're finished putting the cast on."

Max and Mama had just got Grama's things packed, and the ambulance had just pulled out of the driveway, when the Western Union truck drove in. The telegram was collect from Daddy. It said:

BE ON LAST BOAT STOP LOVE, JACK

"Well, that does it!" said Mama, flopping into a chair in exasperation. "Am I supposed to be on the last boat, or is he? The damn fool could have left off the 'Love, Jack' business, and added a simple you or I to give the message a little sense! But Max, if he meant for me to be on that boat, I don't even have time to sit still. They say the ice is coming in early and the last boat to Nome leaves next week. That's fifteen days earlier than the schedule. Let's see, I would have to tell Aunt Lilly I'd be quitting. Imagine quitting an $18.50-a-week job! What insanity!" she laughed weakly. "And of course, Artis and I would need complete winter outfits. Wool slacks would probably be the thing for me and a good heavy snow suit for the baby. Maybe I can borrow Aunt Ganelle's woolies that she mentioned last spring for Jack," she said, muttering to herself as much as to Uncle Max, making a more thorough list as she went along.

"But Max, what am I talking about? Jack undoubtedly means he's going to be on the last boat, or he certainly would have given me more to go on than that! He's probably been paid for the summer's work, and the job is over, that's all. Wouldn't you think so? I wonder how much he's been able to save. Max, if we could just pay a fourth of what we owe, at least they would probably stop calling.

"I can keep my job at the store this winter, and by spring things will have to loosen up a little. Now, let's see, that last boat out of Nome ought to reach Seattle by about the end of this month. I'm sure that's what he means, aren't you?"

The next morning, another telegram arrived:

YOU BE ON LAST BOAT STOP HAVE HOUSE READY STOP
BRING FOOD FOR NEXT EIGHT MONTHS STOP   JACK

CHAPTER 13

Mama called Aunt Lilly first to tell her the news that she would be leaving right away. "Now child, don't get in a tizzy. We'll miss you here at the store, but we'll manage. Now about this food business. I think you're very wise to plan to take what you need with you. They charge a terrible price up there for everything, and you might just as well use the space you're allotted on the boat. You know your Uncle August and I packed in to Dawson Creek in 1900, and I can help you a little on what's needed in the way of non-perishables. Come on out to the store and we'll see what we can fix up."

Aunt Lilly and Mama made up lists all afternoon. Having to buy groceries for a three-day camping trip always had her baffled up to that time, so at Lilly's suggestion they wrote out a typical week's menu, meal by meal. Then they multiplied each item used by about thirty-two, as there were approximately thirty-two weeks between the last boat in September and the first one in June.

"Now all we do is add all the staples we can think of, and we've got those thieving Alaskan storekeepers outfoxed. August can buy most of this stuff direct from the wholesale house, and have it delivered right to the boat. And never mind about the bill, Alice. We think you're a pretty good risk. I know you'll pay when you can. Ninety-nine per cent of the socialites in Normandy Park owe us three times that much. You may as well join the illustrious list.

"But Alice," she added, "what on earth are you going to do about Sara?"

"Max called me about Grama this morning and I think that problem, at least, is solved. The neighbors are all complaining about the racket the chickens are making at their place in town anyway, so Max said he and Ella and the kids will move out to the ranch with Grama for as long as we want them to stay. They need a bigger place anyway, so they can move in right away, and take care of Gram when she comes home from the hospital. Dr. Kintner says she's doing even better than he expected, and the only thing worrying her now is how we can possibly get along in Nome without her."

"I'll see to it that all the family visits her at the hospital regularly," promised Aunt Lilly. "Sara's going to miss the baby so much anyway. And Ganelle's already called Reverend Attebum from Grace Methodist. He'll be calling on her too.

"Now, what about clothes, Alice. I hope you're not neglecting evening shoes and you'll need three formal gowns at the very least."

"Frankly, Aunt Lillian, my thoughts had run more to snow suits and long woolies. I never was the clubwoman type, you know, and Jack and I certainly don't go in for much of the social life, even of Nome," answered Mama.

"Take the long underwear and the slacks, by all means, girl. When we were at Dawson Creek they would have thought we were queer if we'd had the sense to wear long pants in that terrible cold, but times have changed. But definitely, Alice, take some nice things you can dress up in. You've no idea how these small Alaskan towns are. I saw Mrs. Welty at the Sourdough Picnic last summer and she said she and Jake were staying outside two weeks extra especially to have some formal dresses made for her. They have the bank in Nome and are considered one of *the* families. Be sure to say hello to them for me when you get up there, my dear."

Aunt Lilly made it sound as simple as a jaunt down to Portland, but it was anything but a gay departure when Mama and I left the following week on the old S.S. *Victoria*. The Alaska Steamship had been having difficulty filling the first-class cabins, so had promoted a special tourist cruise up the Inside Passage as far as Skagway, across the Gulf of Alaska to Seward, and then on to Nome. The ship was newly painted, the brass polished, and the officers looked scrubbed and hospitable as we came aboard. It was a perfect excuse for the ladies to wear their fur coats and for their husbands to start drinking. By the time the Purser called, "Last call! All's ashore's going ashore!" the ship was one huge floating party.

"Bon Voyage!" called Uncle Max, at the other end of the coiling serpentine. And Mama said she decided right then and there that we would have a "Bon Voyage," even if she did just give up a good job, and we owed eight months' grocery bills, and had left the Seattle credit managers without so much as a good-by. All the money that Mama had been saving that summer for a payment to Elliott Bay Lumber Company went to pay for our clothes and tickets, and so our bridges were badly burned. We would enjoy the next two weeks as if they were our last. No one need know that her snappy fur-seal-trimmed leopard jacket was left behind by a careless Bootlegger's girlfriend, or that my under-wear was homemade by Grama out of old dishtowels.

At this point I decided to stay in Seattle after all. I was afraid of the noise and all the strange people, and I didn't like the smell of the boat and the harbor. "I want to go home. I want my Grama! I don't want to go to Nome!" I wailed. After almost three months, 'Daddy' was a rather vague theory anyway. I even offered to go and live with Uncle Max and help take care of the chickens if we could just go home again.

But the enormous whistle blew again until our ears hurt, and we began to move ponderously away from the pier. The beautiful colored serpentine broke, strand by strand, and lay coiled on the deck, while Aunt Esther and Uncle Max grew smaller and smaller. Finally we could barely make out the spikey outline of the Smith Tower, and then there was only the open ocean to watch.

The Pacific Northwest produced one of its dazzling Indian summers that fall. The Captain took us very close to the Cana-dian shore in the deep passages so we could appreciate the wilder-ness at close range. Many times we could hear the voices in the evening as we passed by a native fishing village, and Mama and I made it a point to be on deck early in the morning to watch the deer staring curiously at us from the forest's edge.

The second day out, Kurt Nordstrom's wife, Helga, introduced herself to Mama at lunch. "Kurt wrote me that you and your little Artis would be on the same boat, so I asked the Purser which table was yours. My Janet [Helga said "Yanet"] is just six this fall. I'm sure the two girls will get along well together. And how nice it will be to have a friend already when we reach Nome."

Helga was right. Janet and I had wonderful times together on the boat. She was a lovely little child with tiny features and tawny red-gold curls and I considered her the "big girl." Janet was always in motion; giggling, running and talking, while I was more the sensible, motherly type. Mama never had to worry about us when we were out on deck, because I would crowd Janet flat to the wall, away from the railing, to keep her safe from the water. When all four of us were on deck, I was in a continual panic that one of them might fall overboard, because I couldn't hold all six hands at once. But most of the day, Janet and I entertained each other playing Sunday School or mothering our doll families in the large Social Hall.

Mama could tell right away that she and Helga Nordstrom were going to be good friends. There was no style to Helga's flat Swedish face, or to her broad practical figure. She was a plain little woman who would be invisible in a crowd. But when you knew her, the goodness of Helga lit her face like a Lucia Bride with a crown of gleaming candles. Sarcasm and meanness were so completely missing in her that she didn't even recognize them in others. All the time we knew her, I never heard her criticize another person, and no matter how hard her life was, she looked forward to the next day like a child waiting for Christmas.

So any misgivings we might have had about Nome were soon swept away by Helga and the S.S. *Victoria*. The cruise director soon had everyone relaxed and happy. He organized a costume ball for the first Saturday night aboard, and the costumes created by the wealthy vacationers were stunning. Many of the women wore real jewels and all their feathers and furs.

Helga and Mama knew they couldn't compete with such splendor, and being the only women without husbands in the party, they decided to go as Mutt and Jeff. Helga was just the right size to fit perfectly under Mama's arm. She had packed a couple of Kurt's long underwear union suits, and over these they wore a pair of new denim strap overalls that Mama was bringing up for Dad. The Purser supplied them with false mustaches and a bowler for Helga and top hat for Mama. Janet and I were delighted with the effect, and our two funny-looking mothers had quite a time convincing us that we were not invited to the costume ball, too.

By the time they got us tucked into the bunks, everyone had arrived at the Social Hall, and the waltz contest was under way. So Mama swept Helga out onto the dance floor, and the Judging Committee was theirs! Count Barkavitch eventually fell heir to Mama's prize for the best-dressed man at the ball—a box of fine Havana cigars. But Helga wore her rhinestone tiara to the social functions of Nome for years afterward.

Even the weather co-operated to make a perfect trip for us, and the sea was as calm as though we were gliding along Lake Washington. The head dining-room steward, formerly a chef from the Empress Hotel in Victoria, made every meal a joy. Helga became a crony of the chef; and often, as the other diners struggled along with ham and eggs for breakfast, our table in the corner was served sweetbread-and-mushroom omelettes, Swedish pancakes with lingon berries, or perhaps a crusty broiled lamb chop.

Waiters were very plentiful in 1933, so there was one man in constant attendance for each table. Our Canadian boy outdid himself to serve us. The table setting usually included a bouquet of chrysanthemums, and sparkling crystal, beautiful linen and silverware spread to the point of confusion. The seafood cocktails always arrived at the table with flecks of ice still on the cup, and the soup was always just the right temperature.

After two weeks of this, we were convinced that Alaska must be even better than the travel folders showed, and I was glad I hadn't stayed with Uncle Max and the chickens after all.

On the day of our arrival, our mothers had us dressed in snow suits and out on deck so we wouldn't miss the first sight of Nome, long before breakfast. By eight o'clock it was much too warm for snow suits, and we began to smell Nome long before we could see it. None of us mentioned it.

No one could eat much of the last delicious breakfast aboard the ship, but it took about an hour to say good-by to all the friends we'd made, and for the women to trade addresses and promises to write soon. By the time they redressed Janet and me in cooler outfits, the ship had dropped anchor about two miles off Nome, and the lighter was coming to take in the first load of passengers. It was a hot day already and the sea and sky had a greasy, tarnished look.

As the steel barge slid out toward us, Mama recognized Daddy standing at the front. "Look, Helga, Jack's come out to meet us. That's him in that wild-looking fur hat, the one I told you about that goes with the plush coat."

"Yes, I can see him now, and that must be Kurt next to him. Sure, he always needs a shave, just like I told you, Alice."

They held Janet and me up to the rail. "Look, there's Daddy on the big barge, see?" But we were both unimpressed.

As soon as the barge was secured to the ship, the crew lowered a special gangplank and Helga and Mama and Janet and I were the first passengers off. Kurt lifted Helga into the air in a bear hug, and soon they were chatting away in the perfect privacy of Swedish.

"Jack, we could recognize you from a mile away by that terrible hat," Mama laughed. It was good to have something to laugh about so she could cry a little and not have it show. "Look, baby," she added, lifting me into Dad's arms, "Here's Daddy. Of course, she remembers her daddy."

But I was too embarrassed by all the emotion and squirmed to get down.

There was so much to say, they had to start on the little things. "Sure I'm fine, Alice. I didn't want to worry you is why I didn't write you when I hurt my leg, that's all. How about you? And the baby—how long she looks! Kind of skinny, isn't she?

"And I've got a *house*, Alice. It's sort of a dump, needs a good cleaning, but we've been working too hard to do much with it. You see, when we found this big vein of gold, at last, we had a big early snow just a few days later. We were all out there digging and sluicing like crazy, when this big snow dumps down on us. About three feet of the damn stuff, all over the machinery, dredge, sluice boxes and all. We had a real hell of a time finding our way back to Nome. Then the day before yesterday, this warm wind sets in, sunshine and all, so things are really in a slush out there.

"As soon as we get you and Helga settled, Kurt and I have got to get back out to the creek and get the machinery put to bed for the winter. Because next spring, Alice, *next spring* we're going to haul the gold out of that creek by the bucketful!"

"But Jack, next spring is a long time from now! What are we going to do until spring?" asked Mama.

"Now just relax, girl. We've got the rent paid till May and you've got the food for the next eight months. St. George says Gust and Kurt and I can each clear about eight hundred dollars for this summer's work, and I'm sure I can get some kind of a job this winter."

"Eight hundred dollars. . . . Oh, Jack, what a beautiful sound that has!"

"Beautiful is right! St. George has the nuggets and gold dust in number-two coffee tins. And wait till you see it, Alice. It's like . . . ."

"No, Jack, I'm not even going to look at it. To see that much money would probably make me want to roll in it. We'll just take our share in a nice, dry impersonal check. That way, we'll never miss it when we send it down to the boys in Seattle."

CHAPTER 14

The lighter was still about a mile offshore when we began to smell Nome again. At first it was only rotten fish stink, but as we came in closer to the beach, it was a combination of fish, hung on long wooden racks to dry in the sun, the mess from hundreds of Husky dogs, rotten fish guts thrown out on the sand for the tide to take away, and the open sewers of the town. I tried to crawl under in back of Mama's coat to escape the filthy air, but Daddy only laughed at us.

"You'll get used to the smell, girls, and anyway as soon as the next freeze comes, Nome will be as sweet as you please. You see, the ground never thaws deep enough to dig sewers or garbage dumps. So, old Swenson has to come around to each house to collect the stuff. Then he hauls it off in his honey wagon to the beach, and the garbage scow takes it out far enough so the tide takes it away."

The sun was high and hot as we approached the beach at Nome. The lighter headed toward a long narrow pier that stretched out from a group of corrugated tin warehouses about two hundred feet into the water. Everyone in Nome who could walk must have been standing lined up two or three deep along the Wagner Commercial Company Pier to meet the boat. A few of the men on the pier called to friends on the lighter, and those on the lighter called back self-consciously.

At first it seemed all the people looking us over so carefully were roughly-dressed men, but then we began to recognize a few women's faces. There was even one woman with a hat on. I still kept both hands over my nose, as we glided past the three or four hundred people, toward the warehouse. Here in the shade of the building was a crowd of Eskimos. They seemed to be sitting in family groups, all watching with open curiosity as the men made the barge fast to the dock. Men, women, and children were all dressed in gay calico parkas and fur boots, trimmed with bright rickrack and beads. Most of the women had sleeping babies stowed easily in the back part of their parkas. They wore wide leather straps pulled tight above their breasts and down under the seats of the babies. The older women kept a casual watch over the larger children, while they laid out their ivory carvings and mukluks for display on intricate fur pieces. None of the men were over five feet tall, but they looked very sturdy and healthy. The native people seemed genuinely happy to see the newcomers, and all along the line we could see their broad white teeth as they smiled at us.

Daddy and two other men caught the lines thrown from the dock and slipped them securely over the cleats. The crowd moved down toward us as the passengers stepped onto the gangplank to the dock. Gust was waiting on the dock for us. "Here Missus, I want you to meet my friend, Florence Beck. She has been our cook this past summer, but no more." He beamed at Daddy. "Ya, that's right, Jack. She's *my* cook now. Flossie and me are getting married this coming week next."

Florence Beck was blushing and flustered as a seventeen- year-old girl as Dad pumped Gust's hand and told him what a sly devil he was, stealing the best cook in Nome. St. George added his congratulations and then was introduced to Mama and Helga Nordstrom.

"So nice to meet you, Mrs. Palmer," he said. "I presume the old boy's told you about the good news out at Cripple Creek. I don't know what we'd have done without your husband this summer, and we're all looking forward to a very prosperous season next spring.

"It's so good to have a few wives around to brighten up the dreary winter coming on. I do wish my Ellen could be here too.

But let's try to get together soon—bridge or something you know. And both of you ladies be sure to let me know if there's anything I can help you do in your moving and getting settled."

"And here's some more nice people I want you to meet, Alice," Daddy said, leading us over toward one of the Eskimo groups. "This is the Aloruk family. Anna, this is my wife, Alice, and my little girl, Artis."

A woman of about fifty, sitting in back of a semicircle of beautiful fur mukluks stood up and took both Mama s hands in her tiny ones. She smiled till her eyes creased closed, and when she talked Mama had to bend down to hear her.

"Oh, Mrs. Jack Palmer, my family gives much thanks to your man. He is help all the summer. He pull in great wood with the yellow car, enough for our fire to last two winters coming."

"That's all right, Anna. It was nothing. I was glad to do it," said Dad. "Joseph and Anna made their summer camp fishing on Cripple Creek, so when I'd make a trip to Nome, on the way back I'd haul a few stumps of driftwood for them, and Anna's been keeping me in mukluks ever since," said Daddy, pointing to the elaborately decorated fur boots he wore.

"Why, Anna, they're lovely! Do you make these all yourself?" asked Mama, running her fingers over the intricate mosaic of fitted fur pieces.

Anna laughed until her shoulders shook. She pointed at her broad, short teeth, and we could see they were worn almost to the gums from chewing the tough leather that makes the soles of the mukluks. "Anna make too many muk-luk. Pretty soon stop!" She seemed delighted at the joke on herself that her teeth were almost gone.

I was fascinated by the tiny woman who was not too much taller than I was, and was just beginning to examine the tiny fur shoes that Anna wore, when the woman in the hat picked her way delicately through the Eskimos.

"Mrs. Palmer, I am Elva Thorlakkson, and this is *Reverend* Thorlakkson. We have the Church in Nome. Mrs. Welty, that's the banker's wife, told me she knows your aunt, Lillian Zeller, in

Seattle, and what a fine woman she is, and all. We're so glad to have you in our fair city, and I wanted you to know that it's not just a bunch of Eskimos here!"

Her strident voice was shocking, coming out of such a pale, plump woman. Her face was white and soft as raw bread dough, with brown snail-shell curls framing her sloping forehead and cheeks. She and her shadowy husband both held their hands together in front of their stomachs and smiled like undertakers.

"And this is your *darling!*" She leapt at me and smothered me down in her black, fur-collared embrace till my cheeks were pressed against my teeth and I could hardly breathe. "I have a *precious* at home just your age, sweet!" she yelled into my face. "I know you and Precious will be perfect playmates. There are so few little white girls for Precious to play with."

Anna and Joseph Aloruk had become deaf. They reset the mukluks in a semicircle and polished some of the already gleaming ivory walruses.

Mrs. Thorlakkson dropped me abruptly and turned her smile away. "Now, we'll be expecting you at the first Ladies Aid this coming Wednesday, Mrs. Palmer. Oh, uh . . . and you too, Mrs. Nordern. We do a great deal for the more unfortunate, you know, and besides, you might as well get in with the right girls."

"And Mrs. Zeller from Seattle wrote Tessie Welty about your poor mother's accident. How is your mother, dear?" she asked solicitously.

"Well, a hip-fracture is fairly serious in an older person, Mrs. Thorlakkson, but . . . ."

"*Wonderful!* Well, we'll be seeing you on Wednesday next then!" She refolded her hands, the Reverend tipped his black hat solemnly, and they were gone.

"I can hardly wait! How about you, Helga?" asked Mama.

"Now, you can't tell, Alice. He seems very nice, probably a fine preacher, and I'm so glad there will be a Sunday school for the girls."

"Why sure there's a Sunday School," protested Daddy. "What do you think this is, a hick town? And wait till you see this baby light up on Saturday nights! There's no place like Nome! You have to see it to believe it. In fact, we might as well make the grand tour right now. What about the Front Street route, Kurt?" said Daddy, picking up a suitcase in one arm and me in the other.

"Ya, I guess that would be the best way, all right, since Front Street is the only one we got."

Most of the people were still on the pier waiting for the lighter's next load with the rest of the passengers and the freight, so we had the town to ourselves as we carried our suitcases and bundles around to the back of the warehouses and started up the main street.

This was Nome. It looked like a drunken, leering, leaning old derelict from the Skid Road. This was a town that had lived high and lusty thirty years before. These streets had held twenty thousand people in 1900, most of them looking for gold and some of them finding it. They were big, hard-fighting, hard-living men and their fancy women. They weren't the type to waste any time building sound foundations or fine homes. They were in Nome to make their stake and get out. After seeing the main street, so was Mama!

It must have been a drunk who laid out Front Street. The narrow board-plank path meandered between two wiggly wooden sidewalks, sometimes barely wide enough for a car and then broadening out again for no good reason. The small one-story buildings were all a scaly gray, each one leaning at a different angle. Daddy explained that the ground never thawed deep enough to dig a foundation, so people merely set their building on the top like toy blocks to shift and lurch with the thawing and freezing of the ice. The courthouse swayed far to the left and hung out over the sidewalk like a sick old man, and we walked a little faster under its over-hang. On the ocean side of the street most of the houses held each other up fairly well, but the sand had been sucked out from under their pilings by the tide till they all leaned backward on their haunches as if they'd been smacked in the face.

We had to watch the wooden sidewalk carefully, as it was built up to two or three feet off the ground in places, and the loose and missing boards showed a small river running underneath. "Down to meet the boat" said a sign on the open door. At the next corner were the Palace Theatre, the *Nome Nugget News*, the Hotel, and the Kougarok Grill, and a combination post office and fire house. This last was an antique valentine of a building, trimmed in crusty, gray wood lace. There was even a tower on the top, which leaned far over toward the sea. Apparently someone else had been worried about it falling into the street, because the top of the steeple had been looped off raggedly, revealing an empty black cavity.

"Here's our house, Helga," said Kurt, pointing to a flat beach-cabin type of place next to the spiky Post Office.

"Well, well. It looks just fine, Kurt," said Helga.

We made arrangements to meet the next day, and Kurt started carrying in suitcases. He ducked down into the small closed porch and in through the front door. "It will surely be easy to heat with such a nice low ceiling," Helga said valiantly, as she went in.

We walked up past the Wagner Commercial Company and General Store, and on to the more residential part of Nome. Here Front Street veered off away from the beach. Our arrival seemed to be the signal for the dogs to start their welcome. Two or three frenzied wolves leaped at the end of slender chains from each yard to snap their long white teeth and howl. One group would hold their note for as long as possible, and the next bunch would start as we passed by. Daddy took the heaviest suitcase and gave one of the dogs a clout that should have crushed in his obvious ribs, but the animal only pulled back his snarling lips and strained harder at his chains. Mama and I felt we were surrounded by the starving beasts, but somehow none of them got loose, and we turned off Front Street onto Broadway.

It must surely have been a satirist who named our street Broadway, as it was merely an alley, barely wide enough for three people. The street wavered along about half a block and then puttered out into the nothingness of the tundra and low-rolling foothills behind the town.

"Here we are, ladies. This one right at the end of the street is ours—the only house in Nome with a tree!" said Dad proudly. It was a crazy, wall-eyed-looking house with the windows all of different heights and sizes, and the roof, like a thatch of stiff, uncombed hair, was tin spotted through with patches, and patches over the patches. No. 14 Broadway, built on short pilings, looked like a tall, skinny, frightened old lady standing on a chair holding her faded gray skirts about her knees, to avoid the melting snow that formed a good-sized river rushing down Broadway.

Up through the mildewed moss in front of the old house, a scrub willow was trying to grow. Someone had planted it next to the boxlike porch which protected the front door, but the willow had edged around to one side of the porch and was pressed against one of the side windows. Every leaf was stripped off.

We leapt over the Broadway tributary, and up onto a meager enclosed front porch just large enough to allow the swing of the front door. When our eyes accustomed themselves to the dim room, we felt we all should be wearing gauze masks over our noses. The place had never been painted, and the walls were infected with large open sores of molding wood caused by the constant freezing and thawing. The uncertain sunlight reflected off the melting snow in through windows that hadn't been washed for years, if ever, giving the room a jaundiced, yellow glow.

From the layout of the rooms, it was plain that the house must have been conceived in haste, and born unloved and unexpected. Then, as new people had moved in, they had merely added another shed as they needed it, or torn down a hunk when they didn't.

We walked down several steps into the bedroom, and I suggested that we better go back to the boat to sleep. The brass bed was a beauty, with spokes and pipes and little round balls, and claw feet, but it was caked with the dust of thirty years and the springs sagged almost to the floor in the middle. Two fat plush Victorian chairs had mildewed and dried till the velvet looked as if it had been cooked, and the springs stuck out at odd angles.

At one time there had been gilt wallpaper, rollicking and gay, but now it hung from the walls in strips.

The kitchen, however, had never had any pretense of glory. It was a room planned by men, merely a place to stew coffee and hang wool socks to dry. On one wall four orange crates were nailed up for cupboards. The few broken cups and cracked dishes inside were partially covered by gray rags tacked to the boxes. In one corner was a small wood-and coal-burning stove, and in the other, the sink. This consisted of one five-gallon oil can, which would serve as kitchen sink, wash tub and bath tub. Fresh water . . . ten gallons, twenty- five cents.

Dad carried our suitcases in and stacked them in the living room. He looked hurt when Mama insisted on a complete Lysol wash-down of the house before we unpacked anything. "My God, Alice, I cleaned this place thoroughly when I signed the lease on it, and that was only a month ago!"

Nevertheless, she spread a clean sheet out on the bed and placed me in the middle, warning me not to move off of it.

Daddy was obviously relieved to get back to the simple world of mining men. "We'll get back about noon tomorrow, Alice. We'll really pitch in and get the place in top shape." And then he was gone.

That was when Mama started to cry. To me, this was like the Rock of Ages itself giving up the ghost, and I was more sure than ever that we should proceed back to the S.S. *Victoria* and thence to Seattle with all possible speed.

"No, baby," gasped Mama, "everything is going to be fine. I'm just a little tired, that's all. You can sleep with me tonight, and tomorrow we'll get some Lysol first thing, and you can help me clean house."

CHAPTER 15

However, the warm weather held, and Dad and Kurt stayed at the camp at Cripple Creek for over a week, finishing last-minute jobs and preparing the permanent machinery for the coming winter. Although Helga and Janet were the only people we knew in town, we didn't have time to be lonely.

I was immediately discovered by the ten-year-old twins down on the corner of Broadway and Front Street. They were both at the mothering stage, and delighted in taking me with them all over Nome and showing me off to their friends. This gave Mama an excellent chance to wash down the old wreck Daddy had found for us. She attacked one room at a time, and by the end of the week could unpack the trunks and feel fairly sure that the bedbugs wouldn't move in on us. By Friday, Mama had made several trips "downtown" for shelf paper and cleaning supplies, and was surprised to find that everyone she met knew who we were and most of our life history.

"Oh sure, Alice," chatted Mabel Wagner at the general store, the Wagner Commercial Company, "Your Aunt Lilly wrote Tessie Welty a couple of weeks ago that you were coming. And of course, Jack told us all about both you and Artis. I saw Elva Thorlakkson giving you the works down at the boat last week, but I hope you'll come to the next Ladies' Aid meeting anyway. All the girls get together and rake over anyone silly enough to stay home. Everyone's anxious to look you over, and besides, it's my day for the eats, and I make the best cake in town!"

Mama met the banker that Aunt Lilly had told her about as soon as St. George gave her Dad's check. Old Jake Welty looked like a tough customer if you were on the wrong side, but as soon as she deposited the eight hundred dollars they were old friends. Of course, by the end of the next Ladies' Aid, Tessie Welty had everyone in town informed precisely on our financial status.

There were no secrets in Nome. Once the last boat pulled out, the main pastime in the little town was finding out what everyone else in town was doing and saying and thinking; and then discussing it thoroughly with all the others. But Mama and Daddy never minded the gossip. Almost everyone was friendly and interested, rather than malicious. We've always been the type of people who forget to lock the doors and pull down the shades, anyway. In fact, Helga and Mama soon felt as vitally concerned as the rest of the ladies about Mabel Wagner's hysterectomy, and "Leaky Pete's" placer mine finally paying off, and Anna Aloruk's youngest daughter being "in trouble" again.

The first two nights in town Helga and Janet stayed at our house for dinner and then spent the night. But by that time the Nome women knew that our men were gone to Cripple Creek and that we were alone. After that, we were invited to a different home for dinner every evening until Kurt and Daddy returned.

They had only been back from the camp for a few days, when we found a large, bulky package on the front porch one morning. We hadn't seen Anna Aloruk since we'd arrived in Nome, but apparently she'd been busy. In the package were two beautifully made parkas. The one for Mama was soft squirrel pelts, trimmed in diamond-shaped pieces of white and black seal, and the smaller one for me was a lovely blue-white fur which Dad identified as winter reindeer fawn. It was trimmed in a great ruff of white wolverine around the face and hem.

Mama knew that the Eskimos usually got around twenty dollars for a good parka, and was quite worried about how we'd pay Anna for her work, but Dad reassured her, "Anna and Joseph won't take a thing. I tried to pay her for the mukluks all summer, but she insisted they are forever indebted to me for those few

loads of driftwood I hauled for them. We'll just have to do something nice for them instead, somehow."

It didn't take long, however, to see that the white people in
Nome had very little to do with the Eskimos. The natives had
their own village across the Snake River from Nome, and Mama
soon found out that the only time it was socially acceptable for
them to come to the town proper was when they had money to
spend, or if a white family had some menial work for them to do.

Of course, there were always the "squaw men," as the town
called the white men who took Eskimo wives. The many men
who took a native girl in to live with them until she became pregnant, and then left her to shift for herself, were regarded with
tolerant amusement by the good people of Nome. "Boys will be
boys," they chuckled. But if the man married his Eskimo girl,
then it was considered a mistake.

As for the "illegitimate" half-Eskimo children, they were
invisible. The Eskimos cared for them and sent them to school,
and chose any last name they happened to like. Often the native
family would name the half-Eskimo child after a prominent
member of the white community that they especially respected
or liked, never after the man who was the real father. In fact, after
Daddy's summer of hauling for the Eskimos, he took a lot of rib-
bing from the men when Anna named her latest granddaughter
Unalakleet Palmer.

But the children of the "squaw men" were an embarrassment
to the whole town. They had to be taken into the white school
and Sunday School, they had to be in the Christmas plays and
the Fourth of July parades, and worst of all, they were so often
beautiful and clever! They had to be dealt with harshly to make
them feel the outcasts they were believed to be.

Mama found out at my birthday party that winter that the
customary way was to invite only white children, but she was
determined to have Anna and her grandchildren too. So rather
than offend the ladies of the town, she had two parties.

The first party, with Janet Nordstrom, Precious Thorlakkson,
the two Welty boys, Sue Ellen Dunninger, and myself, was a

nightmare, as usual. We were snowed in by then, and of course, we all had to be inside all afternoon. Sue Ellen got sick on the third piece of birthday cake, Precious and the two boys had a fight over a candy cane, and I was in tears by the time they left at three o'clock. ("It was really only two," admitted Mama, "but I couldn't stand another minute of it. I set the clock an hour ahead, and sent them all home.")

The next afternoon Anna arrived right after lunch with her six youngest grandchildren, and the new baby, Unalakleet Palmer. As soon as Anna got the parkas and gloves and snowy mukluks off, Mama settled all of us on the kitchen floor blowing bubbles with wooden pipes and jars of soapy water. The native children were delighted with the delicate colors of the magic, floating bubbles. Then Sara, the oldest girl, read stories out of one of my books until it was time for the food. This Sara was one of the homeliest little girls imaginable, but I vowed I loved her "almost as much as Grama," and Mama often had her come over after that to take care of me when she and Daddy went out to the many social functions of Nome. She had a flat, aboriginal face, and her pig-tails skinned back, slick as seals from her low forehead. But worst of all, one black slanting eye looked one way, and one the other. Mama suggested to Anna one time, after they got to be good friends, that there was a free clinic in Fairbanks where Sara's poor walleyes could possibly be corrected, but Anna was definitely not in favor of this plan.

"Sara can see fine, Ah-leece. Teacher at mission school say she is best reader. And Joseph he say this way white men not look at her. Sara is O.K. with funny eyes."

So, while Sara read, Anna and Mama took turns holding Unalakleet Palmer, who was a soft, brown dumpling who slept most of the afternoon, and didn't cry at all. In fact, one hardly would have known there were any children in the house except for the hilarity when they first tried the ice cream. Only Sara had tasted it before, and the rest of the shy little faces were amazed. At first, they were convinced Mama had given them dishes of snow to eat, but when they found it tasted sweet and slipped off their fingers, they all got the giggles and polished off almost the whole gallon.

Anna explained that the Eskimos made ice cream of sorts too, but theirs was a mixture of fresh blueberries and seal blubber. They poured this mixture into seal pokes and buried it down in the frozen tundra to be brought out during the winter as a rare delicacy.

Shortly before dark, we put caps on all the jars of soap suds and wrapped them with the bubble pipes for the children to take home. Anna herded them into their outdoor clothing, and each child stepped up shyly to thank Mama for the party and the "magic water," as she and I promised to come to Unalakleet's party next.

However, the Palmers weren't the only ones who appreciated the Eskimos. Jimmy Roach was one of the best known "Squaw Men" in Alaska. He'd been active in Nome politics for years, and how the old man loved to talk about his experiences. Like many a good storyteller, he did some pretty fancy embroidering, but most of his adventures were at least based on fact. He lived only a few blocks from us, so during the winter when there was nothing else we could do anyway, we saw a lot of the old man.

Jimmy Roach had been shipwrecked off the coast of Nome on a whaling schooner in 1890, and never quite made it back home again, home being County Kilkenny, Ireland. He never did find any gold, but he made a lot of money during the gold rush with his three saloons at Candle, Alaska.

"You see, Nome was then in the way of being the big city, while Candle was sort of the wild mining camp," he explained to Mama, one of his favorite listeners. "During the All Alaska Sweepstakes dog races, the teams had to go from Nome to Candle and back, and before anyone was eligible for a prize, they had to be registered as having reached one of me three places—The Castlecomer, the Coothill, or the Belturbet. They was my gold mines, so to speak. Oh, I always kept my saloons nice though. No women around or nothin' like that. And on Sundays if we'd happen to have a priest or even a preacher in town, or even just a good talker, we'd curtain off the bar and have a service."

But then Jimmy married an Eskimo girl and got his "cause." He took it upon himself personally to save the Eskimos' reindeer herds from "thim dirty theivin' bastards of Whitfields!" In fact, he became such a fanatic on the subject that he never did much else beside his "reindeer work" for the rest of his life. He gave speeches (to which no one listened), wrote pamphlets, and organized drives (with only his native wife and six half-Eskimo children as members). For years he tried to keep the reindeer for the Eskimos, until he was one of the town's oldest jokes.

No one laughed right to his face though, because almost everyone liked Jimmy. The government had imported the reindeer for the Eskimos as food and also as an industry for them to work at so they would be self-supporting in the increasingly complicated economy brought in by the white people. This seemed to be a successful idea, and the reindeer thrived on the tundra around Nome.

But then John Whitfield and his son discovered Alaska. They came from Prince Rupert in about 1915 to hunt seal in the Pribiloff Islands. They spent their first season out on the Islands slaughtering four times as many animals as they could possibly bring back in their small boat. Then they sold their catch in Nome and blew the whole profit in one slavering drunk that lasted until a week after the last boat sailed for Prince Rupert. It was that winter that the old man and his son discovered how much easier it was to cheat the unsuspecting Eskimos out of their reindeer herds, than to work for a living.

They opened a dirty little office down on the beach and called it the Whitfield Native Crafts Company, which was supposedly in the benevolent business of preserving and promoting Eskimo arts and crafts. They kept a few pairs of dusty fur mukluks and some clumsy examples of ivory bracelets and other ivory artifacts in the window, but no one in town had ever heard of a sale being made. When the tourists came in on the boats in the summer, both Whitfields closed the store and spent the days in the Blue Fox so they wouldn't be bothered by any customers.

Instead they would wait until they heard of a native family in financial trouble, of a father in jail or a family deserted and without food. Then they would move in and trade a boxful of cheap staple groceries or a few bottles of watered rot-gut whiskey for the Eskimos' share of a herd of reindeer.

So, in less than twenty years, the Whitfield Company had cheated the trusting natives out of their reindeer, and butchered them by the thousands for their thriving fertilizer factory down in Prince Rupert in Canada.

But years of defeat and disappointment didn't seem to stop Jimmy Roach. He wrote letters to Eleanor Roosevelt and Mahatma Ghandi, to Aimee Semple McPherson and Secretary of the Interior Harold Ickes, to Congressmen and kings, to anyone who would read them and to lots of others who never bothered. Of course, he never had much money, but he did everything any man could do to help his friends.

Old Jimmy was starting off on his rounds one morning at our house with a coffee and cake breakfast, when Anna Aloruk came running into our front yard and banged on the door. The night before had been a real blizzard, and at 10 A.M. it was still almost dark. The wind had drifted the snow a couple of feet up against the door, and Dad had to push against it to get it open. Anna brushed past him without her usual polite greeting and hurried into the kitchen.

"Quick Ah-leece," she said, still out of breath, "get some hot-cold water. I have a baby!"

To our amazement, the old woman carefully placed a small newspaper package on the kitchen table. The papers were stiff with drifted snow, but as Anna peeled them back and opened a thin cotton blanket, we could see the tiny brown face of a two-or three-month-old baby. For a minute we were all too stunned to say a word.

Anna threw back the hood of her parka and put her wrinkled cheek down next to the baby's naked chest. "She lives! Quick Ah-leece, get water and oil!"

Old Jimmy sprang to the range to build up the fire, while Anna and Daddy moved the table closer to the heat. "Open the door to the oven, Jimmy. And Jack, look upstairs in the medicine

box for some baby oil or olive oil. Top drawer of our bureau!"
ordered Mama.

While Mama mixed hot water from the teakettle with soap
flakes, Anna opened the baby's blue lips and blew her breath
directly into its mouth, pressing the tiny chest in and out gently
with her hands. By the time the soapy water was ready, the baby
was breathing and began to flutter its eyelids slightly.

"Alice, I can't find any oil except this hand cream. How's
that?" asked Daddy as he ran down the stairs.

"Oh no, it would have perfume in it . . . might burn her skin.
We'll just have to use uh, . . . the Wesson oil. That'll do."

Anna had the crisp, frosted papers peeled away and the
blanket laid back. The plump baby was dressed in a filthy calico
diaper that was frozen to her skin wherever it touched against
her, and her tiny hands and feet were quite blue.

Daddy and Jimmy were just bumping into each other and
getting in everyone's way trying to help, so Mama sent them
down to Wagners' for a baby bottle and nipple. Anna held the
baby by the arms and head while she sponged the frozen diaper
away from her skin, first with the warm soapy water, and then
with the Wesson oil. The baby whimpered a little as the cloth
pulled away, but she was too weak to cry. The buttocks and thighs
and soft, round stomach were burned raw where the diaper had
frozen to her, but Anna found the cornstarch and had covered
her with a fine layer of it by the time Jimmy and Daddy got back.
The two women left the baby completely naked and covered her
first with a fine old cotton undershirt of Dad's and then a clean
sheet torn in half.

"Ah, there's the little sweet doll," cooed Jimmy at the baby.
"You should have seen Mabel Wagner when young Jackie and me
asked her for a titty bottle. The old girl would've given her *eyes*
to find out which one of us was hatchin' out a baby on the sly!"

"Where did you come by the young thing, Anna?" he asked.

"Oh, she is my cousin's," said Anna vaguely." She was drunk
too long, and the older kids come to my house this day early. Say
Mama doesn't come home, where is baby. So I look in snow by

Blue Fox place. Too far to cross river to home, so I bring 'em here to Ah-leece. Pretty soon after the milk, I take baby to my house. She's tough, eh?" laughed Anna.

"But Anna," Mama protested, "you haven't got room for another baby in your house. There are so many already, and where are you going to boil the milk and clean the bottles and the diapers . . . ."

"Ah-leece, you make too much work," chuckled Anna. "My last girl has still a sucking baby. She will feed this one too, easy!"

"But Anna, this baby should be taken care of by its parents. The mother ought to be put in jail for doing a thing like this. And who is the father?" demanded Daddy.

"Well, not too sure. But she is my cousin, and baby is so small. Joseph and me, we *like* to have her. A sister for Unalakleet Palmer."

That seemed to settle the matter, so Mama mixed some canned milk and boiled water for the bottle, and fed it to the baby while Anna muttered darkly about feeding a child with such a hard, funny-looking thing. But the baby gripped on to the nipple with all her strength, and didn't stop sucking till the last drop was gone.

Anna said she could easily take the baby home herself; but Mama dug out some little sweaters and warm blankets that I had outgrown, and insisted on walking home with her to help with the packages.

The Aloruk family had heard them coming and were all out on the front porch to meet them—old Joseph, two daughters and their husbands, a son and his wife, and eight assorted grandchildren. "Quick Joseph, the coffee for Jack Palmer's woman! She helps too much for the new baby!"

The young women must have just prepared lunch for the family, as there was a pot of some kind of fishy-smelling stew in the middle of the kitchen-living room floor. After Joseph put the coffee pot on the back of the stove, he and the young men and children all squatted around the stew pot and dipped in with hands and large soup spoons. Anna insisted that her friend sit down too and have coffee. "Eat if you are hungry, Ah-leece, but the white ones make a sick face at seal blubber," the old woman said, pointing at their stew. "*Ikiyuna*, they say. Stinks!" She held her nose and made a funny face, while the Aloruks and Mama laughed.

The only furniture in the main room was the stove and a large oil can for a sink. Then in the next room were four wooden beds covered with fur pelts, but Mama said she knew the new baby couldn't have landed in a better spot if the Federal Bureau of Indian Affairs had picked the home themselves. As she left, the youngest daughter, Grace, was nursing little Rosie, as Joseph immediately named her when Anna showed him the little pink burned bottom, while poor Unalakleet Palmer had to yell a while for her lunch. The way the Aloruks ogled and raved over Rosie, you would think Anna had brought home a sack full of gold nuggets instead of another hungry mouth. So that was how the Aloruk family got their last baby. In six months no one knew or cared that she wasn't just another one of Anna and Joseph's grandchildren.

CHAPTER 16

As the winter months slipped away, we really began to like Nome. Winter covered the dirty little town with soft, white pillows of snow, and just as Daddy had predicted, even the smell disappeared. Especially in the winter, Nome was more like a large group of friends living together than a town. Helga and Mama were both committee chairmen in the Ladies Aid, and both Janet and I loved school. Officially I wasn't old enough. I was only four years old, but Mama had me coached to say I was "near five," and it worked. Jimmy Roach and many of the other old-timers entertained us for hours with their stories of the past, and Mrs. Wagner promised to teach Mama how to make her special spice cake as soon as the eggs were ripe enough. Mama felt she was *in*!

All the kids in town trooped in to the Sunday School, which was only a few blocks from our little shack on Broadway. Elva Thorlakkson kept the children and herself busy learning "Jesus Loves Me" and the Ten Commandments, and we all had a wonderful time.

But one morning a few weeks before Christmas, when I got home from Mrs. Thorlakkson's primary class, I had to let them in on the facts. "Mama, there's no Santa Claus! It's only Jesus's birthday, and Santa Claus is just something they make up to tell kids!"

As Mama stripped off layers of parka, gloves, coat, ski pants, mukluks, sweater, and wool socks, I felt smaller and smaller, and the lower lip began to go down as I added, "I guess it must be so if the Sunday school teacher said, isn't it, Mama?"

She hauled me onto her lap and told me, "Why baby, I'm surprised at Mrs. Thorlakkson. Poor lady, she just doesn't know any better, that's all. But you know there's a Santa Claus, Artis. Why, you even sat on his lap last Christmas at Frederick and Nelson. Remember when you ordered the pink tricycle from him? And you got it, too."

The sympathy got to me, and I began to wail. "But Mama, they don't even have a Frederick and Nelson here for Santa Claus to come to. And Grama's not here, and we had to leave my tricycle at home. Even if there is a Santa Claus, I don't think he would come to Nome!"

Daddy heard me crying, and when Mama told him what Mrs. Thorlakkson had said he scooped me up in his arms and sat me on one of the chairs in front of the large window. "Why the old biddy! What's the matter with a woman who would do that to a bunch of four-and five-year-olds?"

"Just look out that window, Pooky, and you can practically see Santa's workshop from here. We're only a few miles from the North Pole, just about in the old boy's front yard. Why, girl, you couldn't ask to be in a better spot at Christmas than Nome. He's got so many toys to stuff in that sack of his to take to all the kids, that sometimes by the time he gets to Seattle, most of the choice items are already taken. Or sometimes the reindeer go around the corners so fast, the toys fall out and get all bunged up. And sometimes there's no snow down south and the poor critters have to work so hard to pull the sleigh they can hardly make it. But *Nome*, well that's a different story! To his team he gives a whistle and away they all go like the down of a thistle, and where do they land first? Right here, of course. And you know what he's going to have for Old Lady Thorlakkson in that sack? A great big collection plate full of tacks, especially for her to sit on!"

This picture delighted me, and with the help of the frosting dish to lick, I was happy again. But during the next week, Mama could tell that my faith had been seriously shaken. She heard me talking to my favorite doll at bedtime. "If you dare to say there isn't no Santa Claus, you won't get nothing but a plate full a' tacks! To eat!" And I slammed him into his bed.

Mama began to worry about Santa Claus too, as the cold clamped down harder and harder. The snow stopped and even the wind turned off as the temperature went down to thirty-seven degrees below zero that week before Christmas. Dad had a job by that time, working as building foreman on one of the Alaska Road Commission's projects, but it was impossible for the men to work outside in that cold. Even with an inner ruff of wolverine fur to guard the face, the men's breath would collect on the fur of their parka hoods and turn to ice needles. Unless they wore double gloves, which made working almost impossible, nails or any other metal would freeze to their hands. So Daddy, as well as most of the other men in town, was home that week.

By the day before Christmas, he was telling Mama how to keep house more efficiently, and she was telling him what was the matter with his relatives. It became very plain that week how the old miners managed to shoot each other every so often when they were snowed in together.

"Jack, I read in the *Nome Nugget* that Wagners' have Christmas trees for sale. Why don't you and Artis take a trip down and look at them?" suggested Mama. We were both eager for the idea, and quickly struggled into our complicated cold-weather outfits. Then Daddy slipped me up inside his parka and held me up so only my nose and eyes peeked out at his neck.

"O.K., you look like Mother and Daughter Kangaroo. Now, remember, tell Mrs. Wagner you're just looking. Those trees are probably sky high! And while you're gone I can get the p-r-e-s-e-n-t-s wrapped."

By the time Mama got a pair of fur-lined gloves and a suit of practical white woolen underwear wrapped for Dad, and a snow suit and paper dolls for me, she said she felt even more lonely and low. She stacked the presents one on top of the other, and then tried grouping them casually against the base of the oil heating stove, but they still looked like only four little packages.

Of all the years, thought Mama, when Artis should have a wonderful Christmas, this would be the one when all we can afford is a snow suit and some paper dolls! She would know that there was a Santa Claus if she could come downstairs and find a lovely doll with eyes that close and a little tea set with roses, or a green velvet coat trimmed in fur, under a feathery Christmas tree.

But Mama gathered up the four small packages to hide them out in the "cache" thinking she'd like to just leave them there permanently. She knew I wouldn't venture into the cold, dark room, but Daddy always was a peeker and shaker, so she put the gifts down in back of some old wooden barrels in the far corner. They didn't seem to rest evenly, and she groped around until her fingers touched a long, narrow book of some kind. She replaced the packages and took the little book into the warm kitchen to see what it was.

On the first slightly molded page of the old diary, in an old-fashioned spiky script, was written:

Christmas Thoughts in Nome City

Chas. L. Guimond
December 24, 1900

The bells are tolling the joyous tidings announcing to the world the anniversary of the Birth of our Saviour; Joyous tidings to some, but sad and lonely recollections it will bring to others in this land of darkness. Sitting in my lonely cabin as I write, I am one of several thousands more. Shall I tell you what they think about? I will endeavor to do so with one sweet word . . . HOME!

Oh, blessed is he who on this Christmas Eve can enjoy the comforts and happiness of home, surrounded by his loved ones. Think, my dear reader, who so happens to read these lines, of the poor lonely one who is spending his Xmas day in a lonely cabin upon the bleak and dreary shores of Cape Nome . . . away from the ones he loves and who love him. Will he ever see them again, his loving wife and angel children? Or is he doomed to die upon these dreary shores . . . a lonely man in a Cape Nome cabin? (Time will tell!)

Pray for his return to his beloved ones. Like Thousands more, Dame Fortune, with her alluring golden visions, tempted him to leave to seek fortune in Alaska. He left his home, intending to return in time to spend Xmas with the ones he loves so well. But instead of fortune, he, like thousands more, met disappointment. And as he sits in the stillness of his Cape Nome Cabin, he breathes a prayer to the angels in Heaven that they may spread their protecting wings over his loved ones, and they may be spared to enjoy many a Merry Xmas and a Happy New Year.

Just then Mama said she heard Daddy and me stamping the snow off our feet on the front porch, and quickly rinsed her eyes with cold water. She knew that if I saw her tears over the quaint old diary I would be sure that Santa Claus was dead.

"Make way for the woodsmen, gal," shouted Daddy. "We just chopped down this enormous noble fir Christmas tree!" He stomped into the kitchen with the tree over his shoulder, the tiniest, scrawniest pipsqueak of a seedling that ever lived. But both Daddy and I felt we had pulled off such a coup, that Mama didn't have the heart to ask how much it had cost.

"Mama, Mrs. Wagner said it's one of the prettiest trees in Nome, and Daddy got some tangerines and a bed—and a surprise secret, and we're going to pop popcorn to string on it, and . . . ."

Daddy laid the meager thing on the kitchen table, while I danced around it like a moth. The limbs of the tree had been tied to the trunk for so many weeks that it looked as if we would have to use lead sinkers to weight them down. The top branch had had some type of wound in its formative years, and was undecided as to which way to lean, so it compromised by angling first one way and then the other.

But Mrs. Wagner had me convinced, anyway. I thought it was a lovely tree. After a lot of discussion, we decided the best place for the tree was in front of the big window in the living room, "so folks can see it going by, and just in case Santa Claus does go over, he'll see the lights in the window."

Daddy and I popped and burned and strung corn, while Mama set up the little tree on the coffee table. She had several long strands of crystal beads that we wound around the branches to weight them down. Then came the popcorn strings, and six tangerines stuck in close to the trunk. We wired about twenty pale green birthday candles onto the tips of the tiny limbs, and the Shirley Temple paper doll in her best pink ballet outfit served as the angel on the top. Daddy was still struggling with the birthday candles, which had a tendency to flip over, taking the branch over upside down with them, when Helga, Kurt, and Janet Nordstrom peered in the window at the tree.

"Hey, you're early," Mama said, as she opened the door and lifted Janet in. "I haven't even got the ham in the oven yet."

"Well, here's the Christmas bread. It can go on top of the stove to keep warm and the dessert in the cooler," said Helga. "You stick the ham in, Alice, and I'll just see about this darling little Christmas tree. Just like the old country it is with the real candles! Why Artis, I think it is the prettiest tree I've ever seen!"

"Sure," I admitted, "even Mrs. Wagner says so."

"But Helga," said Kurt, winking broadly at Daddy, "You didn't tell the news. We've all got to hurry right away down to the I.O.O.F. Hall. Santa Claus is coming to town!"

Helga drew Mama into the kitchen, while Janet and I squealed around the living room, trying to put on all our outdoor clothing at once. "Yake Welty was around this noon, Alice. They've got old Swenson's sleigh all painted white and cleaned sweet as a flower, so you'd never know it was the same old honey wagon. It's full to the brim with presents for every child in town, Eskimos and all. They herded in eight reindeer off the tundra, and Swenson into a Santa Claus suit, and then he will drive them right down Front Street up to the I.O.O.F. Hall to give out the gifts. But we've got to hurry. They say they will let the animals loose at three sharp."

Each mother caught one little girl and stuffed her into snow suit, parka, mittens and mukluks and started down Broadway, toward Front Street. The huskies were howling furiously at the noise and laughter of people converging from all over Nome. It was almost completely dark by three in the afternoon, so each group carried a bobbing flashlight or lantern to pick their way through the snowdrift trails.

Everyone in town was out to see Santa Claus, and by the time we neared the I.O.O.F. Hall, people were walking four or five abreast down the narrow channel cut through the snow. Mrs. Moritz even put a sign in the Post Office window, "Gone to see Santa Claus! Back in an hour."

As we went by the Blue Fox, the town bachelors, warming up for Christmas Eve, came steaming out to join the crowd. The mellower group, who'd been there since shortly after breakfast started a whooping rendition of "Little Town of Bethlehem," and pretty soon all of Nome was singing. We stomped our feet to keep warm, and puffed and snorted like a troop of horses, while everyone called back and forth to each other. "Deck the Halls" was next and then "Jingle Bells."

Anna and her family stood with the rest of the Eskimos at the edge of the crowd until Daddy spotted them, and shouted across, "Hi Anna, Joseph. Bring the kids over here by us on the steps where they can see Santa Claus when he comes." Soon all of Anna's grandchildren and "cousins," which included every Eskimo family in town, were seated on the steps of the Hall, chatting excitedly with the other youngsters.

The children from the primary grade Sunday School were called upon to sing "Silent Night, Holy Night," and then Mama said it really was Christmas Eve. Everyone joined in for the second chorus, even the old miners who probably hadn't sung since the days of the Golden Gate Hotel Songfest Jubilee in 1903. But their cracked old voices blended in fine with the uncertain lyrics of the Eskimos, and the Blue Fox drunks, and the Presbyterian Senior A Cappella Choir.

Mrs. Thorlakksson was putting Reverend Thorlakkson into position on the steps for a few words, but old Swenson beat him to it. We heard Jake Welty's whisky tenor come in loud and clear from down at the very end of Front Street. "O.K. Let 'er rip, Saint Nick!" he bellowed.

And eight wild reindeer who'd never been off the tundra or seen a human being were given the flick of Swenson's whip, and were off and running straight down the main street. Each reindeer had his own notion of escape, but the high drifts on either side of the street kept them tunneling straight down the street. The sleigh slewed wildly from one side to the other of the sheet ice, while the reindeer skidded and shrieked in terror. But Swenson was having a magnificent afternoon. He stood leaning back against the reins, cursing gaily at the animals, sled, and people, and his curling beard and hair flew back from his face. Jake Welty had staked him to a bath and shampoo at the Finlandia Steam Baths, and he never looked lovelier, before or since.

Mama was sure that the reindeer, sled and all, were going to grind straight into the group of children, but six or seven of the young men surrounded the snorting animals and stopped the sleigh. Santa Claus had a large new shovel stowed in with the gifts, and while the boys held the panicky reindeer, he shoveled out the presents onto the steps, calling out all the names he could think of.

Janet and I and the rest of the children were too amazed to speak. We watched dumbfounded, as if God himself had come down to earth, and the adults had to press the packages into our hands and fold the fingers over. I was a little disappointed that Santa Claus didn't have anything for Mrs. Thorlakkson, as I was looking forward to that collection plate full of tacks that Daddy had told me about.

But with the last gifts shoveled out, Swenson leapt back into the chariot, to his team gave a whistle, and away they all flew like a steam locomotive! Janet and I settled back down to earth gradually as Kurt and Daddy carried us home on their shoulders. We had one last ride around the front yard piggyback, as Helga and Mama scurried to arrange their gifts and ours under the little tree. There was a very fancy, store-wrapped one already there for "Dear Mama, from Artis and Daddy."

Shirley Temple got a little singed from one of the candles, but Kurt dunked her in his water glass and she was saved. I found the lucky almond in Helga's special Christmas rice pudding, and was quite worried at Kurt's prediction that I would be married within the year. Mama looked kind of astounded when the store package turned out to be a feathery pink bed jacket, but other than that, it was a perfect Christmas.

CHAPTER 17

It was an ice-still night in January when Mama and Daddy were awakened by the night watchman on the Road Commission job. He pounded the door until they both stumbled downstairs through the quiet, cold house to let him in. Archie told them that the heavy snow of a few hours back had weakened the new foundation, so Mama made a pot of coffee while Dad hurried into an extra pair of longies, shirt, wool pants, sweater, two pairs of socks, mukluks, hooded parka, and fur mittens. The two men slupped the scalding coffee and hurried away, looking like two fat, dark snowmen against the moonlit snow. Mama watched out the window as they ran down the street to keep themselves warm.

The night was alive and quivering with a cold that seemed almost tangible. It was thirty-five degrees below zero, and Nome was never more beautiful. The moon was a round dime of silver, and each star glistened close enough to pick. All the mean ugly shacks and rutty streets were softened with a puffy glaze of snow. Not one sound broke the stillness . . . even the ever-present breakers of the Bering Sea were frozen, and it was strange not to hear them. Not a breeze interrupted the perfect night, and it might have been a night on the moon by the look of the deep blue shadows on the snow.

Mama had been back in bed only about an hour, failing to warm her feet or stop worrying over the trouble on the job, when she heard a faint singing away down the street. She looked at her watch to see that it was about 2 A.M., so it could only be a drunk.

"Way down upon the Swanny Rivah,
Far, far away,"

It was not loud or uproarious enough to wake anyone; just happy, sentimental drunk singing. She giggled to hear the funny guttural voice go on to, "That's where my heart is yearning ever . . ."

Mama didn't turn on the light as she didn't want to attract his attention, but looked out the window to watch his lonely serenade. As he ambled slowly down the middle of Broadway, wobbling first to one side and then to the other, Mama recognized him as Big Tom. Tom was the well-known half-Eskimo in town, who was supposed to be the son of Big Thomas McGrath, the man who made the first strike in Nome in 1898. She knew it was Big Tom immediately because of his size. He stood about six feet tall—for an Eskimo, a giant. There wasn't another native in town over five-two. But what Tom gained in size from his white father was made up for by his typical Eskimo features. He could have lumbered out of one of those prehistoric ice caves, by the look of his sunken eyes under heavy hooded brows and sloping forehead. His nose was flat on his face and either nature or fate had smeared his mouth in a continuous stretched smile.

However, he was always easygoing and overly polite to Mama. Dad had put Big Tom to work on several jobs where considerable brawn was needed, but as soon as he was paid, he always went on a prolonged spree. It was hard for the half-Eskimos to find work in Nome, and the fact that Daddy treated Tom as a human being endeared him to the big man forever. When he was sober, Tom was much too shy to say more than a polite "Hello, Mrs. Palmer," and that with his big arms hanging down, and a painful blush on his face. But with a few drinks under his belt, he was "Big Tom," and often came visiting, asking for his friend, Jack.

But during all Tom's benders, Mama had never seen him this uproarious, and she was glad she hadn't turned on the lights. He continued his song, "That's where my heart is yearning ever, Far from the old folks at home!" The lonely lyrics must have done the trick. Mama was horrified to see him turn into our yard. Of course, the door wasn't locked. No one locked doors in Nome. She was immobilized for a moment while she fought the desire to crawl back into bed and pull the covers over her head. But I was sleeping in the next room, and there was no doubt that Tom would come looking for Dad upstairs if he found the house below empty. She didn't take time for robe and slippers, but raced through the hall and down the stairs leading to the front door. She threw herself against the door, reaching for the unfamiliar lock, wondering if it worked . . . and the door opened.

Big Tom stood there in his oilskin pants and a wool shirt, close enough so Mama could see the beads of sweat on his smiling face, only inches from her own. The cold air came in with him and struck through her thin nightgown, right to her heart. She tried to hide behind the door, but he pushed it further open and stumbled into the room. It was still dark in the house, but she could see him clearly by the light of the moon on the snow outside. His face was greasy, and he had a bold "Big Tom" smile.

"Tom wanta see Jack," he demanded. His eyes wouldn't focus and his breath stank of fish and sour wine.

"No, Jack's sleeping. You can't see him now, Tom," Mama managed to squeak out. "You come back tomorrow morning and see Jack then."

The smile disappeared, and the native took on the look of the Neanderthal man they show in anthropology books. "Tom wanta see Jack," he said, louder this time. He slobbered a little, and took a step closer to Mama with his large hands raised.

Mama didn't think consciously of what she had to do, but moved as a cornered animal would. She put both hands on his broad chest and shoved with all her strength and almost two hundred pounds. Usually it would have been like shoving a mountain, but as it was, Tom was both completely surprised and very drunk. He staggered backward through the door and off the edge of the porch. Mama's hands were shaking so that it seemed to take hours to lock the latch. Then she ran down through the black "cache" and into the bathroom to lock the back door, fully expecting to meet him coming in. But she got that locked too, and ran upstairs to the hall window where she could see the front yard. Her plan was to yell for help from there, but by then everything was so still, except for her heart banging against her ribs, that she couldn't do it. Then she saw Big Tom again, lying in a snow bank that had formed at the side of the porch directly below her, just where she'd pushed him.

He lay very still for about fifteen minutes, while Mama wondered how long a man could live in such cold, and what they gave you for manslaughter. She knew if he stayed in that snow much longer he would freeze, but was at a loss to know what to do about it. The only house close enough to yell to was the Thorlakksons' down the street. She knew the sparse minister and his wife could do nothing to help her anyway, so she decided to wait another few minutes. As she watched the still form in the snow she made her plans.

"I decided that if he didn't get up within the next ten minutes I would lock the door to Artis' room, sneak out the front past Tom, and run the three blocks to the police station. I brought out all my outdoor clothing into the hall so I could watch the Eskimo while I dressed."

She was just putting on her mukluks, when Tom started to move. He wallowed around in his own trough for a few minutes, and finally crawled up onto the porch. Mama's heart started to gallop again. . . . He could have easily broken down the old door. But he only shook himself like a big dog, and wobbled his way down the steps and out of the yard. He plunged through the snow to the street and away he staggered, yodeling faintly, "Far from the old folks at home!" until she could see nor hear no more.

When Dad got home about 6 A.M. he was surprised to find Mama sitting up, fully dressed, drinking coffee at the kitchen table. He was even more amazed to hear her shaky story. As usual, he made a great joke of Mama's jittery condition, and referred to Tom as "Alice's boyfriend" for weeks afterward.

It was only a few days later when Anna stopped by with a new pair of mukluks for me. She had some cake and coffee while Mama told her of her wild night with Tom. Anna didn't think it was at all funny. In fact, she actually turned pale and took Mama's hands in hers when she said, "Ah-leece, this was a very bad thing. Big Tom is a very bad man when he is drunk."

But by then Mama was ready to make light of the thing, and told Anna it was all over and not too much to worry about. Later that afternoon we saw Tom shoveling the sidewalk in front of the jail, and knew that he had "made the can" again, as they say in Nome. He peered out shyly from under his eyebrows, smiling and bowing, "Good morning, Mrs. Palmer." She could tell that he remembered nothing of his late visit to her. He was so tame and peaceful looking, it made her feel foolish to have been so afraid.

But on another still January night about a year later, Big Tom was drunk again. The men said he left the tavern singing, and in only a shirt and pants. Only this time he went back to his own shack. The snow was deep, and again the ice had stilled the breakers, and no wind blew. He picked up his Eskimo wife and carried her far out on the ice where it was thin enough to chop a hole through to the sea. There he took the small woman and held her under the water until she stopped fighting, and didn't come up any more.

So Anna was right. Big Tom was a very bad man when he was drunk.

CHAPTER 18

Always the biggest party in Nome (and Nome was a town of very big parties) was the Nome Sweepstakes Dog Sled Race, usually held around the end of February, depending on the weather. This was a great event in the little town where the winter seemed so endless and the isolation from the rest of the world so complete. Some of the best teams in Alaska were trained and kept right there in town, and drivers and dogs came from all over the Territory to race in Nome.

The race was the high spot of the year; not only for the dog sled men—the whole town turned out. This was an event to be studied and plotted on and talked about all year; but by a month before the races, bets began to be laid, wild claims of speed and timing boasted of, old friendships broken and patched and re-broken, and widespread frenzy reigned.

At the Blue Fox there was at least one fight every night over whose lead dog was the smartest, and even the Ladies Aid bridge circle almost split up that winter over a difference of opinion on whom they should sponsor for the Sweepstakes Beauty Contest, which supplemented the race, along with the Eskimo Dances and Blanket Toss, the Church Pageant, Band Concert, the Men's and Ladies' Ski Race, and countless private tapering-in and tapering-out parties.

No one seemed to know exactly when the first dog sled race had been run in Nome. Jimmy Roach said there had been a big race in Nome every winter that he could remember, which was a long ways back. And of course, the Eskimos had always raced their dogs for sport. Their very lives depended on their teams. The dogs were their only means of transportation in the winter, the best way to hunt reindeer, and the only way they could visit other villages. The dogs even served as a food supply if things really got tough. Anna assured Mama that a nice fat puppy of three months or so was a delicacy, especially in winter when fresh meat was scarce.

However, the winning teams were almost always owned by white men rather than Eskimos. The natives cared for their dogs as well as they did their wives, sometimes even better, but they simply didn't have enough food to spare to keep a team in good shape all through the winter. By March the native teams were usually so starved that they ran on pure viciousness rather than the spirit of competitive fun. Joseph Aloruk usually had to get out in front of the team and hold his gun as if he were going to shoot some fresh meat for them to eat before his team would stir their bones to run.

The Palmer family was especially excited by the races that winter because Millie Bergdorf had just given us a beautiful all-white Siberian Husky pup named Podunk. Like all of our dogs, it hadn't taken him long to find out that Mama was a pushover for a handout almost any time of the night or day, that Daddy spoke dog language fluently, and that I was inclined to dress the poor thing up and play "mothers" with him.

Podunk was about nine months old when we got him, and technically he was supposed to stay in the kitchen, but that rule didn't last long. He liked Daddy's chair, the blue armchair with the good view of the front yard. Whenever Dad came and found Podunk in his chair, he'd have great fun luring him out of it by pretending he heard something outside. He'd knock on the wall behind him and rush to the window.

"What's that, Pody boy! Who's out there?"

And of course, Podunk would fly out of the chair, the fur on his neck bristling, and dash to the door to be let out to check the guard. It always worked, and each time Daddy would settle into his chair while Podunk sniffed furiously around the yard. He could always take a joke though, and would come panting in, tongue hanging out in a lopsided smile.

One evening after dinner, Daddy beat Podunk to the chair, so the dog settled down contentedly by the kitchen range. He was only there a few minutes when he started to thump his tail and whuff softly. Then he ran to the window nearest Dad, and barked hysterically out into the dark. Next he ran to the door and demanded to be let out, barking and whining all the while. Of course, Daddy got up and went to the door to see who it was, and Mama even left the dishes to look too, only to see Podunk calmly back away from the door and trot over to the chair. He hoisted himself up, circled carefully a few times, and plopped down, eyes shut tight and a fatuous grin on his face.

So everyone in town knew that we had ruined Podunk as a sled dog, of course. But the racing fever had bitten Daddy, until not even Millie Bergdorf could talk him out of entering Podunk in the Year Olds' Singles race.

"Listen, Jack," said Millie, sensibly, "All that pup has been trained for is to pull one of Artis' doll buggies. If you're really serious about racing Podunk, let me put him out with my team for a while and toughen him up. He's one-eighth wolf, you know, and I'm sure he could take it."

But the idea of putting our baby out with Millie's pack of snarling, gnashing professionals was unthinkable. So, with only a short month to go, Daddy, Podunk, and I went in training. The dog was at the height of adolescence, and took the whole thing as a good-natured romp in the snow. Daddy had borrowed a small, lightweight sled from Joseph Aloruk, and the plan was for me to sit in the sled as ballast while Dad worked with Podunk to get him used to the harness and the idea of running with the sled.

But Podunk was too interested in the smell of the other dogs on the leather, in teething on the delicate harness, snapping playfully at Dad's mukluks, and sniffing at every snow bank. Daddy finally got the big fool squashed into the intricate harness. He was sweating and swearing by this time, but the dog took it all as a funny joke. His pink tongue lolled out one side of his mouth and he tried a tentative chew on one of the sled runners in back of him.

"Now baby, you just sit tight, right where you are," Daddy said, tucking the fur lap robe around my knees in the sled. "I'll stand in back and 'mush.'"

In short races, as were held in Nome, the first start has to be right, because if the dog stops, the runners will freeze to the snow. The driver stands in back of the sled, holding the handles, and runs along for a few seconds to give the sled a good start, a little like a boy with a scooter. Then he jumps on the stand at the back. The inside of the sled is used to carry gear and supplies or additional passengers.

In the long races (every few years they held a sled race from Nome to Fairbanks that sometimes took ten or twelve weeks to run) there were very strict rules as to how many pounds could be carried in the sled and also limits as to what this ballast could be. But, as was so often the case, in Nome anything goes. Most of the old sourdoughs threw in a sack of flour and a couple of cases of beer for the trail, while others preferred a nice Eskimo girl.

As for Podunk, I'd always been his playmate before, and he couldn't get the picture that *I* was supposed to sit in the sled, and *he* was supposed to pull it. He wanted to sit in the sled too, and by the time Daddy was stationed at the handles in back, Podunk had scrambled up onto my lap, reins, harness, and all, licking my face and slobbering happily at this wonderful new game. He looked back at Daddy expectantly and gave two sharp yaps as if to say, "O.K. Jack, let's get this thing moving. I'm ready for my ride."

Mama was watching the spectacle from the front window. Dad looked as if he might cry. There was a little whip in the socket on the right handle, but, of course, he would no more have used the whip on Podunk than he would on me.

"Get out of that sled, you lard!" he yelled, and Podunk clambered over the side and wiggled over to Daddy, in his sideways crab-walk, apologizing profusely for whatever it was he had done wrong.

Finally Dad got the harness untangled, set the dog at the front of the sled, and firmly pointed him in a forward direction.

Daddy stepped on the back of the runners again and snapped, "Mush, Podunk!"

Podunk sat down.

By this time quite a few of the Broadway Street neighbors had come out to see the fun, and Podunk could see that he had a really appreciative audience.

"Mush, dammit," hollered Daddy. And Podunk performed his best and only trick that might have something to do with this strange command of "mush." He sat up smartly, paws together, and grinned and panted for the cheering crowd.

"Hey, Jack," crowed Leaky Pete, "What kinda odds you taking on that champeen a' yours?"

"When you leaving for the Fairbanks Race, Palmer?" hee-hawed another old-timer.

Finally Jimmy Roach took pity on us, just as I was about to cry of embarrassment for Daddy and pity for poor Podunk. "Look, Jack, the wee Amadon doesn't know what the hell you want of him. You must yell 'Mush' and lead him along a bit like this, from the front. I've seen the natives train the young dogs many a time."

So Daddy ran to the front of the sled and took Podunk by the harness, pulling and running alongside. "Mush, boy, mush!"

Now this was more like it. Podunk pulled the little sled skimming along Broadway as if it had wings, while the crowd cheered again. The wind flattened back the wolverine fur around my face, and the little steel runners hissed along the packed snow on the street. We were almost to Front Street before I noticed that Daddy was running in back of us instead of alongside. Podunk had at last got the hang of the thing, and wasn't letting any plod-footed human hold him back.

We slithered around the comer of Broadway and Front Street on one runner, but the robe tucked around my knees kept me from falling out. By this time Daddy and Jimmy Roach and several of the others were almost a block behind us and losing distance fast. All I could see ahead at the end of Front Street was the Snake River, black and deep and sluggish with slush ice. Being chicken-hearted as ever, I began to wail my loudest until the regulars at the Blue Fox thought it was the town fire siren going by for sure. Several of them joined the chase.

Of course, Podunk was no more anxious for the Snake River than I was. He was just paying a social call to his former owner and good friend, Millie Bergdorf. We slowed down to about fifteen miles an hour and barely made the comer and front gate of Millie's neatly kept yard. She kept her team leashed just inside the gate and they almost went insane as we crashed in. The lead dog was one-fourth wolf, and wasn't taking any nonsense from a half-grown puppy intruding in his yard. Although Oleson was chained, he grabbed Podunk's harness in his jaws, and it looked as if he was going to hurl us, sled and all, right into Millie's lap as she ran out the front door.

But Millie carried a big stick and laid it on with abandon— one smack for Oleson right in the teeth that sent him sprawling, and another for Podunk that stopped him in his tracks.

I was still howling from Millie's arms when Daddy and Jimmy Roach puffed into the yard. After a short but pithy lecture from Millie on amateurs of one sort and another, Daddy decided against running Podunk in the singles race, for that year anyway. It only took two rainbow popsickles at Wagner's store to get rid of my hiccups and to convince me that we didn't have to mention *all* the details of the ride to Mama when we got home.

Even without Podunk the family was to be conspicuously represented at the festivities on the day of the race. Elva Thorlakkson had been lashing the whole combined Sunday School classes onward and upward for the pageant to open the Nome Sweepstakes celebration, titled *Welcome Spring.*

"It's a cinch the whole affair could use a little elevating," agreed Mama, "but cheesecloth daffodils? God help us all!"

Elva had sent the whole primary class home with specific instructions, complete from directions on how to make the costumes, and diagrams of the dance steps, to proper spiritual attitude and guidance from the parent. All the kids with talent or even just a lot of nerve had speaking and singing parts. Precious was, of course, the star—The Spirit of Spring—while Janet Nordstrom, with her naturally sweet voice and tap shoes, got to be a bluebird. The boys were elves and toadstools, while the remaining no-talent girls made up a chorus of swaying daffodils. That's all we had to do—sway.

Elva was determined that her part of the show was going to be exquisite, even though the rest of the town seemed to be slipping closer to the jaws of hellfire every day. So we had given up Sunday School classes entirely (except for the love offerings) in favor of practicing for the pageant.

With almost a month to go I was terrified that Mama wouldn't get the costume done in time, but finally with Helga's help, she got the thing stuck together. Janet's bluebird outfit was a perky blue satin jacket and shorts that fit her chubby figure to a tee, while Precious' spirit of spring turned out to be quite ethereal, done in pale blue chiffon bias strips that floated like sixty.

The elves and toadstools were easy enough. Everyone wore long underwear anyway, so all the elf mothers had to do was to dye the little boys' union suits a deep, rather poisonous shade of green. Tessie Welty was left to her own devices on something that would make her twins look like toadstools. "I like the idea of that long underwear myself," said Tessie. "You can depend on it that old Thorlakkson will be welching on the coal, as usual, and the church will be like a tomb!" So she dyed the boys' suits a sickly mauve, just a shade off tattletale gray, and found a couple of small Japanese parasols, painted a matching mauve, to hold over their heads as the roof part of the toadstool.

"I guess they look as much like mushrooms as they ever will," admitted Tilly. "But they'll do all right, just so Elva has the sense to keep them apart while they're on the stage. They fight like a couple of wolves!"

As for the daffodils, all six of us felt that we were really lovely. The bodice of our dresses was a rich yellow satin, and the full skirts of a paler yellow cheesecloth, very stiffly starched and flouncy and very short.

"I realize you want the girls to look like little ballerinas in their tutus, but Elva," complained Mrs. Dumler, "these kids will freeze, with those bare legs of theirs hanging out like that. They'll just have to wear long stockings, that's all. Maybe we can all get the white ones and they won't be so bad."

In honor of the new hardwood floor in the church, Elva had ordered soft-soled shoes from Sears and Roebuck for the whole cast and we were all anxious for their arrival to complete our costumes. In fact, everyone had been wearing their cheesecloth and satin more or less constantly since they'd come off the sewing machines, and they were beginning to look pretty bedraggled. We all had great hopes that the new white shoes would sort of set things up again.

They came in a wonderful big box by air mail, and turned out to be more like tennis shoes than ballet shoes. They were made in Japan for Japanese feet, certainly not my long thin ones. They were fine on the Dumler girl, who was fat all over, but on me, they simply wouldn't stay on, especially not during the tippy-toeing part.

"For pity sake, child, don't cry," snapped Elva. The strain of the big production began to tell on us all. "Your mother can tie them on, or use a little piece of elastic band, can't she?"

The dress rehearsal went quite smoothly, in spite of the squeaking of twenty pairs of rubber-soled shoes on the hardwood. We tried switching to stocking feet, but that turned into a free-for-all ice-skating binge on the shiny floor. And when Sharon Dumler suggested we all wear our mukluks for the "Welcome Spring" number, I thought Mrs. Thorlakkson was going to hit her.

The morning of the race dawned cold and clear—a perfect day for the races, but pretty chilly for *Welcome Spring*. Sure enough, the Reverend was welching on the coal, and at 9:30 A.M. when we arrived to dress we could see our own breath. Anyone with a team in the race was out working with their dogs, and the bachelors and sourdoughs were warming up at the Blue Fox, but everyone else in town had mushed their way through seventeen degrees below with a stiff breeze off the ocean to *Welcome Spring*.

Reverend Thorlakkson allowed himself quite a lengthy commercial on how nice it was to see such a large crowd, but how few familiar faces among them, etc., etc., while backstage the cast went into its final windup. Mrs. Thorlakkson had to play the organ for the senior a cappella group first, so we were left more or less to our own devices. While Elva was swinging into "There's a little Brown Church in the Wildwood," one of the toadstools decided to try out his brother's Japanese umbrella as a parachute and turned it inside out. Everyone's tennis shoes just about drowned out Mrs. Dumler's rendition of "Spring Song." It was about then that Janet Nordstrom announced she thought she was going to be sick, so Helga, in desperation, herded the whole primary class into the ladies' restroom for a few quick choruses of "Jesus Loves Me" to calm everyone's nerves.

Then, finally it was our turn. Elva was pounding out our cue. The *flowers* that *bloom* in the *spring*, tra *la*!

The daffodils came teetering out, twelve little tennis shoes all squeaking and stuttering in unison, and a wave of muffled coughing and strangled snorts swept the audience. The hard part was over and all we had to do was coast (and sway) while Precious gave her monologue. She was throwing herself into it with her blue chiffon flapping away, when Willy Welty (the toadstool at upper left) started hopping toward his twin brother. He couldn't forget that busted parasol, and he had blood in his eye for sure. It was pretty hard to keep your mind on Precious for a while there, but just as Willy galumphed toward his cowering twin, Mrs. Welty sneaked out from the wings and yanked him offstage without a sound.

Janet Nordstrom was next with "Birdie with the Yellow Bill," and was doing beautifully, but the daffodils were all in trouble of one sort or another. We'd been swaying for about ten minutes and were all stone cold, for one thing. Sharon Dumler was yawning and sighing and I was sure they could hear her stomach growl clear in the back row, while the girl next to her was having a terrible time with those fantastic harnesses we had to wear to hold our socks up. One long white sock had collapsed to the ankles and the other was bound to go if she let loose. As for me, I was just bored stiff with the whole affair. That starched cheese-cloth had begun to itch. I tried to co-ordinate my swaying with my scratching, but apparently it wasn't too effective a cover-up. Mama and Daddy didn't even dare glance at each other while I was going through these strange contortions for fear they would both break down and howl.

But finally, Janet brought her tap dance to a close to the accompaniment of six sneezing, shivering, yawning, scratching, droopy-socked daffodils; and the applause was thunderous.

"Oh, I liked that little kid in the umbrella the best," guffawed Jimmy Roach, with tears in his eyes. "You know the one dressed as a hoptoad!"

"No," insisted Millie Bergdorf, "Artis and the daffodils were the best, kinda like ostriches with the St. Vitus dance!" Kurt Nordstrom laughed so hard he knocked his folding chair over on the floor with a crack.

"Hey, that sounds like the starting gun. Let's get down to the races!" The church emptied in record time, and the Spring Welcomers all went home to put on ski pants, wool shirts, and sweaters, two pairs of socks, hats, parkas, and gloves.

CHAPTER 19

The Nome Shrine Band had been tuning up at the Blue Fox all during the church pageant, so by 11 A.M. they were really improvising. Although it was only about ten degrees below zero at the judges' stand where they were playing, most of the Shriners had stripped off their parkas. They were all quite red-faced and steaming when we arrived, oomping and thumping fit to bust, and old Mr. Wallach was working on his bagpipes in back of the bandstand, getting ready for his solo.

But best of all, the King Islanders had arrived. They are a remote group of Eskimos who live out on the Aleutian Chain and come into Nome only on very special occasions. They speak only Eskimo, wear beautiful native clothing, and keep all the old customs and culture of the natives—almost completely untouched by modern ways. They had a mangy-looking team to run in the race, and also three weddings to be performed. There was no priest on King Island, so they had to save up their brides and christenings until they got to Nome where Father Murphy could unite the happy couples. All three girls were dressed in gay organdy store dresses, and one even had "high heels behind."

Father Murphy performed the triple wedding at the nine-thirty Mass and the post-nuptials were in full swing by eleven. To the disgust of the Ladies' Aid, all three of the brides pulled off their organdy party dresses right there on Front Street and slipped into parkas for the blanket toss. Daddy put me up on his shoulders and I had the best seat in the house.

About fifteen of the young men stretched a rough circle of some kind of supple, springy hide between them until it was taut as a drumhead. Then the brides rolled onto the thing and were tossed up into the air, higher and higher, to the chanting of the Eskimos who were watching. Although the song sounded like only about three grunted syllables, Anna told Mama proudly, "King folks make this song. Make up own words and music!"

The pretty young girls seemed to be made of all soft muscle, with no bones or joints, as they did their fluid dance, landing softly on the sagging hide and then springing up and turning slowly in the blue sky.

By the time Jake Welty finished his opening address at the bandstand, the dogs were almost crazy. They knew they had been getting ready to race for days, and old Wallach's bagpiping was the last straw. There were at least a hundred Huskies tied up along Front Street, all howling and yapping at once. But they had to wait a little longer. The ski race was first.

"Ladies first!" bellowed Welty into the mike. "Come on, girls. You start right here at the red line when the gun goes off, then down to the end of the river and back!"

And that was the first time we noticed Helga Nordstrom in *skis!* "Now Alice," she laughed, "you don't need to look so surprised. Kurt is so mad, he won't even talk. He thinks I'm going to make a real fool of myself in front of the whole town. But I'm going to enter anyway. I haven't been on skis for fifteen years, but you know, back home in Sweden I was pretty good. We always had to ski cross-country, not for sport but just to get from one place to another. So I'm used to flat-land racing like this. Wish me luck!" Helga took a pole in each hand and made her way slowly over to the starting line, smiling shyly at all the young girls in the race.

"Oh, Jack," said Mama, "poor little Helga. Why, she's the only one in the race over seventeen. I wonder if she can even make it to the river and back."

Jake Welty fired the starting gun and yelled, "Let 'er rip, ladies. And the last one home gets the booby prize!"

The eight youngsters pushed off on the flat course with poles flying and their long legs slapping their skis on the packed snow, while Helga just sort of eased ahead as if she were walking. She looked like a little pack horse trotting along with the race horses.

"Oh, I can't look," I said, hiding my eyes. "Poor Helga is going to get that booby prize!"

Soon all the girls were around the curve in Front Street and then Helga too disappeared, and there was nothing to do but wait. The course was about a mile each way, so the Shriners swung into "Hard-Hearted Hannah, the Vamp of Savannah," while we waited. Janet was hopping around on Kurt Nordstrom's shoulders, but he looked black as a blizzard, until the little girl piped, "Hey, look Papa, there comes old Mama, right down the street, and she's all by herself!"

We could hardly believe it when the little pack horse pulled in at the finish line all alone. She was jogging along at the same even pace she had started, and not even breathing hard, but smiling like sunshine.

A great cheer rose up from the band and the P.T.A. section and the Blue Fox gang and the King Islanders, and even the dogs started howling again. Jake Welty was giving Helga the five-dollar prize and a blue satin ribbon, when the first of the hot-shot skiers began to straggle in with their curls drooping and their shirts coming out of their pants.

Helga and Kurt and Janet come home with us for a hurried celebration lunch, but we were all back on Front Street by one o'clock for the first dog sled race of the day. Daddy had clipped a collar and leash on Podunk and was holding him firmly between his legs as we watched the start of the race.

"Maybe the boob will get the idea from the older boys that the dogs are supposed to pull the sleds, not sit in them!" groused Daddy.

The dogs were almost uncontrollable by this time. They whimpered and snarled and slashed, while the owners struggled to hold them from killing one another. The Shriners had gotten so loosened up at the Blue Fox at lunch that they decided to try "The

Flight of the Bumblebee," in waltztime. It had begun to snow a little, but nobody seemed to mind, least of all the musicians.

When Jake blew the whistle for the one-minute warning, the drivers began to push their sleds into place. Each man had two or three people to help cudgel the dogs into position and to try to keep them from jumping the gun. A track had been smoothed for several miles along the little railroad that ran out into the tundra. Jimmy Roach was stationed at the end of the turn-around place to check that each team made it out before they turned around. It was rumored that he had four bottles of real Irish whisky out there with him, so there was very little doubt that all hands would make it that far at least.

By the time Jake Welty fired the starting gun, we were all as excited as the dogs. Millie Bergdorf's team made the best start, as usual. She snapped her beautiful, hand-tooled whip just above Oleson's ear tips, and they were off and away down the course and almost out of sight before the King Islanders' team knew what it was all about. Finally a couple of the Eskimo men ran out in front of the dogs, pointing their shotguns ahead, and then their dogs started to run too. There were to be three heats of four dog teams each run. Then the winners of each of the three heats would compete to decide the grand prize winner.

In the meantime, most of the town adjourned to the movie house for the Sweepstakes Beauty Contest. They had cleared away the folding chairs down in front so the Shriners could provide suitable music for the event, and as Mama and Daddy and I came in they were tuning up with "Hold That Tiger."

The crowd was boisterous and red-cheeked as they boiled in from outside. Everyone was excited about the race, and right up to the time we found our seats, bets were still being made and changed as to the outcome of the first heat. But still, there was an undercurrent of tension and suspense throughout the darkened theater. Everyone in town had picked their favorite girl weeks before, according to who owed which one of the girls' fathers money, whose mother played in which bridge tournament, and some freethinkers who were more or less uncommitted even chose the one who was the prettiest of the bunch.

Nome didn't often get the chance to see a bathing suit, so when Jake Welty announced the first contestant and Shirley Dumler came out in a daring two-piece number, the voters went wild.

"O.K., gents," yelled Jake, without benefit of microphone, "the decision of the judges will be made according to applause only. No amount of foot-stomping and whistling and hell-raising is gonna make a damn bit of difference. So shut up!"

"The next contestant will be Miss Phyllis McGinnis, R.N., of Nome General Hospital!"

There were ten girls in all, each one violently upheld and supported by one group or another in town. Mrs. Welty had her eagle eye out for everyone who had a loan with the bank to see that they clapped for their Jo Ann, while Elva and the Ladies' Aid gang were howling for Wagner Commercial Company's oldest daughter, Bridget.

Actually, all the girls were young and pretty, but as far as we were concerned, there was no contest. Grace Nenana came on the stage last in a simple black satin suit that matched her black satin hair perfectly. She was a beautiful girl, and as good and sweet-natured as she was smart. Grace was half-Eskimo, had been brought up at the Catholic Mission out on the tundra, and had been working as a bookkeeper at the bank for about a year. From the hooting and hollering from the bachelors in the front row and from the Shrine Band (who were supposed to be impartial), it looked as if Grace had the beauty contest sewed up.

However, there seemed to be some complications.

"Mrs. Welty has been trying to get Jake to let her go down at the bank for months," whispered Helga to Mama. "Tessie says she is too pretty to be a good worker!"

"Ya, poor old Yake is on the spot now," added Kurt. "Look at him sweat. Maybe he knows now how we feel when we ask him for money!"

As Grace stood in the center of the stage, tough old Jake looked imploringly from the crowd of clapping men in the audience to

Tessie Welty, whose gimlet eye had him nailed to the stage, and then back at his daughter Jo Ann, who favored her mother.

"Now this is a very close decision," stammered Jake. "We'll have to have a run-off between Miss Jo Ann Welty and Grace Nenana. I'll leave it right in your hands, folks," he pleaded to the audience.

The two girls came to the center of the stage and Jake held his hand first over the lovely Grace and then over his daughter's head. Convention, and community spirit, goodness and light, the P.T.A., and the Ladies' Sewing Circle clapped hard for Jo Ann Welty, but the rebels belted it out even harder for Grace Nenana. So Jake was still right in the middle-on the spot. The sweat shone on his bewildered face and it was a terrible thing to watch. He was stuttering and switching his head from side to side, like a wounded bull, when his friend Joe Wagner stepped in to save the day.

"Just a minute, folks. We can't have the judging yet. There's one more contestant you ain't seen yet. May I present Miss Kougarok Leona, fresh in off the tundra!"

And from behind the dusty stage curtains simpered Beans Larsen, in a very hastily thrown together outfit made up of a pale salmon-pink union suit, a brief spangled ballet skirt held together at the waist with a length of frayed rope, and a chancy looking brassiere made of two Pet Milk cans. Somewhere Beans had found a large, rather droopy-looking ostrich feather fan which he held demurely, first over his Pet Milk cans and then over his knock knees. His wig was a wild, strawberry blond affair that looked as though it had been made for Harpo Marx, and the enormous mukluks he wore gave the whole costume the right finishing touch.

The band was pretty badly broken up in wild laughter, as was the rest of the audience, but they managed to toot out a few more blasts of "Hold That Tiger" while Kougarok Leona sashayed over to Jake. Mr. Welty knew a rescue when he saw one, and lost no time in naming Kougarok Leona as the winner of the Nome Sweepstakes Beauty Contest of 1935. Jake looked like his old self again, and as he handed Beans the silver cup, he planted a big sloppy kiss right on his whiskery cheek, and then gave him a kick in the pants for good measure.

Beans left his costume on after the show and was called upon to defend his honor and his manhood more than once during the remaining afternoon. He showed up around town the next day with a very bad shiner. Elva and the Ladies' Aid were mad as hatters about the whole show "sinking to such a vulgar display"; and when Millie Bergdorf won the final Sweepstakes Race, it really ruined their day, especially when she donated the hundred-dollar prize to Father Murphy and his mission. But to the rest of us in town, it was the end of a perfect day. Even Jimmy Roach vowed there had never been a better Sweepstakes Day.

CHAPTER 20

....

Early that spring, Daddy had urged Red Collier, the Alaska Road Commission Superintendent in Nome, to hire some Eskimos as his labor crew. This was the first time that Eskimos had even been hired at equal working conditions and wages, and old Joseph, who served as interpreter and general straw boss, let the young men know that it was his friend, Jack Palmer, who was responsible for their good fortune.

The men on Dad's crew were steady, hard workers, and even though they were small, they stood up under the intense cold far better than any of the huskiest Swedes. A problem they never had to worry about with the Eskimos was illness. Either the air was too cold for germs in the winter, or the natives had a natural immunity to protect them, but we never saw a man off work for a cold or a backache, or even a child with a runny nose. Many times women and half-grown children would wade out to their waists in slush ice to help pull in the kayaks, and work in their wet clothing for another hour to unload fish or seal or to secure the boats on the beach, but there was very seldom an Eskimo in the Nome General Hospital. Even their teeth were perfect.

Mama once asked Tilly Eckmann, the head nurse at Nome General, if she had any ideas on the subject.

"No, Alice, I don't know just why it is they're so healthy. By all rights, they ought to be a pretty sickly bunch, living in those little shacks across the river, open sewage and garbage every-where. But it seems as long as they eat their own food, and the men keep away from the booze, and the women stay away from the miners, they're all right."

"I used to come up along the coast with the old Coast Guard Cutter *Bear* about 1901, and then the Doctor and I would mush it from Nome to Candle by dog team to take care of any trouble there. We only got to Candle about every three months, but there'd never be any sick Eskimos. A few white men in the area would be pale and sappy-looking by the time the winter was over, but as long as the Eskimos ate their raw seal blubber and walrus liver, they were fine.

"You know, I've eaten most of the Eskimo foods, and it's not too bad if you're good and hungry. The only thing like that that ever stopped me was one time up around Point Hope. Doc Hammerstorm was with me, and we were headed back towards the ocean to meet the *Bear*, but we knew we couldn't make it that night, so we pulled in with a little village of about thirty Eskimos. They'd been ptarmigan-hunting that day and were really having a powwow to celebrate the catch. So, of course, they asked us to share and we decided to pitch in. Well, they just threw about twenty birds in a big stew pot to boil, feathers, feet, guts and all. And we were so hungry, it actually smelled good. Doc and I stood our turn and watched some of the little kids while they picked through the craws of those birds to get out the willow shoots. They'd pop in the partially digested shoots just like they was candy. Anyway, we stood our turn, and right when my place in line came up, the chief cook gives the whole mess a stir, and dammit, Alice, if one of those ptarmigan didn't just roll over on its side and stare right straight up at me, kind of mournful like! That was too much for me! I lost my appetite, and all the Eskimos in the camp had a good laugh at me and the Doc being such cheechakos!"

"But I suppose that's the kind of food that keeps them healthy. In years past, before they got too mixed up with some of the bums that have been through Alaska, you couldn't even find an Eskimo with a rotten tooth. But of course, once the diseases did get in, the natives would die from flu or measles like it was the Black Plague. Some miners took measles into Candle in 1903, and before we could get the serum in there, I saw whole natives camps wiped out till there was no one left to bury the dead ones. By the time we got the serum, the Eskimos had it figured out that one man could carry the sickness from one village to the next, so they put guards out to keep anyone from getting in or out. Dr. Jenner was on with me that winter, and one time a big Eskimo chief kept us camped just beyond rifle range for two nights and two days while we watched them carry out forty-nine people and bury them in those funny coffins on stilts, six feet up off the ground, so the wolves wouldn't get in. Finally the guard got sick, and we moved in and 'shot' everyone left who could still wiggle."

"Yes sir, the white man's burden is a honey up here, Alice. The ones we didn't kill off early by giving them measles, we kill now with T.B. and syphilis! Ah, the refinements, the refinements!"

There was not an absentee problem among Daddy's native crew, either. In fact, the first Sunday after the boys began working for Dad, we woke up about nine o'clock to find Joseph and his crew waiting patiently at the edge of our porch to be told where to work that day. It was completely beyond their understanding that the white men could waste a perfectly good day out of the precious few of a cold winter. Finally Mama got the idea across to Anna, who had a "cousin" who was reared at a Jesuit mission, that Sunday was "Church day—God's day, not for working." Anna translated the general idea to Joseph, and the next Saturday he told the men the new rule.

"O.K., Jack Palmer. I tell the men your Jesus Christ get 'em if they work on last day after this many," said Joseph seriously, marking off six days in the snow. "Young kids pretty dumb, eh?"

About the middle of April, Dad's Eskimo crew began to show signs of restlessness. Everyone else in Nome had their bets placed as to what week, day, hour, minute, and second the ice on the Bering Sea in front of Nome would break, but the Eskimos weren't allowed in the pool. Gambling and drinking were considered exclusively the white man's sport. Just the same, they were continually looking out toward the sea, listening for the first grinding sounds, and chattering excitedly among themselves.

Finally, one Friday afternoon, the mystery was explained. After work, old Joseph announced to Daddy, "Tomorrow the ice break. Next day we go for walrus. The young men and old Joseph want you for honor. You give us good work, we give you first seat in boat for walrus. O.K.?"

Of course, Dad accepted enthusiastically, and asked what he could bring along for the day's hunt. But Joseph insisted he need bring nothing for the outing except his thirty caliber Springfield rifle. "We will go as soon as it is light. Anna will have parka for you."

Mama stoked Daddy as full of breakfast as possible that Sunday morning, and he dressed in his warmest parka and waterproof mukluks. By that time I was awake and insisted on coming along to see Daddy off. The sun was just beginning to glint up over the broken ice and black ocean, but daylight was still hours away as we reached the native village across the Snake River from Nome.

The northern lights were especially beautiful at that time of year. The cataclysm of the ocean coming to life again and the hurried preparations of the whole village were all displayed against a background of pale, opalescent pink and green and blue hanging curtains of light that shimmered and changed as you watched them.

Daddy was quick to lend a hand in moving the gear needed for the hunting expedition, but Anna noticed that Mama and I were fascinated by the beautiful lights in the sky.

"Watch, little one," she said. "Anna make the lights dance." She put her two index fingers between her teeth and whistled piercingly and loud, and the colored curtains of lights danced before us. The pink faded and became purple, while the green shimmered against the snow even more vividly. A couple of Anna's grandchildren were watching too, and were as delighted at the trick as we were. Soon a group of us were whistling and keening away until the dogs howled and pawed at their ears, while the lovely colors bobbled and parted and shimmered together again.

But as the sun rose higher out of the ocean, it was time to go to work. Anna and the rest of the native women were busily stowing guns and large butchering knives and seal-poke life preservers in a large hide boat called an umiak. The umiak's ribs are carved from Alaska birch driftwood from the beach, and then covered with large ugruk (sea lion) hides. They make a well toward the back of the boat for an outboard motor, and each side is outfitted with about fifteen oarlocks.

The older children were put to the task of blowing up the seal-poke life preservers, and then several of the women sewed up the openings with their bone needles and seal-gut thread. Anna had to stand on a large rock to hoist a transparent-looking skin parka over Daddy's head. The Eskimos make a special waterproof outfit for fishing or hunting on the water out of paper-thin seal gut. It is gathered tight at the face of the hood, and at the cuffs, making a light weight, almost airtight covering. However, on Daddy, the suit came only to mid-thigh, and the sleeves were three-quarter length. Anna knew his measurements, but she could never quite believe that a man could be six foot two and have such long arms and legs. (It was the same with the first pairs of mukluks she made for Mama and me. We even cut paper outlines of our feet for her, but she was sure there had been a mistake in the tracing. It took three pairs of the shoes, several inches too short, and almost as wide as they were long, before Anna could adapt to Mama's size 10 AAAA.)

The women brushed the little children out of the way as the men came down to the boat from a community breakfast in the native church building. All the able-bodied men of the village were there, about thirty in all, and obviously having a good time. They were steaming and red-cheeked from their hearty breakfast, and doing a great deal of laughing and hunters' talk. When they saw Dad in his tiny skin parka, they were delighted with him. Old Joseph shouted with laughter, "I think Jack Palmer get plenty wet if the umiak turn over!" He stripped off his yellowish skin over-pants and insisted that Dad wear them instead. They fitted him like golf knickers, but with two inflated seal pokes strung around his waist, he was unsinkable, at least.

Joseph pointed to a small seat at the bow where Daddy was to sit, and planted himself in back of this, his paddle raised. The men seated themselves in the large clumsy-looking umiak with a minimum of fuss and last-minute instructions from the women. Not one of the ladies suggested going along to show off her new hunting togs. No one said, "Be careful, dear," or "Don't drink too much in the blind!" Anna and the rest of the women merely put their shoulders up against the boat and pushed it out onto the water far enough so the men could paddle, and they were off. The umiak glided over the black water with amazing speed for such a clumsy-looking scow, and soon they looked very small out on the vast gray ocean.

"Anna, don't you worry about Joseph and the others when they go out like this?" asked Mama. "What if a storm should come up, or . . . ."

"No, Ah-leece. Too many *if* to worry about when the men hunt walrus. If the storm comes. If the umiak tip over. If a man fall in the sea. If a walrus goes for the boat. Too much to think. So we go home and make a feast, and wait till the men come home."

Daddy always said that the walrus hunt was one of the most memorable experiences about Alaska. As soon as they were a mile or so offshore, the men began to sing and stomp the bottom of the umiak to keep warm, and also to tell of other hunts they had been on. Like most hunters, each man had his favorite story to brag of and by the time they reached the large floe ice, about ten to twelve miles out, the monsters they had slain were enormous. Joseph was one of the oldest men in the boat and had a hard time with English, but Dad had picked up quite a bit of Eskimo and together they pieced out what the old hunting songs and stories were about.

Old Joseph also explained that Jack Palmer, as the guest of honor and the only white man the Eskimos had ever taken on a hunt, was to have the first shot. No one was to fire until Dad shot his walrus. The old chief warned him that, even though the guns were very powerful, they must break the neck of the animal, or the walrus would carry the shot away with him. The walrus flippers are very small and provide only balance, while his main locomotion is by throwing his weight from his powerful neck and shoulders to his hindquarters. He humps along this way on the ice until he can reach the water, and then he is complete master of the situation. Joseph said that a walrus could have as many as ten or twelve shots in him, but if he could reach the water, the Eskimos gave up.

They slowed the small motor to a sputter to ease in and out through the moving ice floes, when one of the young men at the side of the boat sighted the first walrus a mile away. They were merely tiny dark specks against the white of a fairly large floe, two or three acres across. Immediately, Joseph signaled to the man standing by the well, and he cut the motor and hauled it into the bottom of the boat. The men at the sides of the umiak took the oars and fixed them silently to the oarlocks. The ice floes all about them kept the water smooth as oil, and the men dipped each oar in carefully, sideways, and recovered their strokes with the oars barely above the water so that the drip would be silent.

For a half-mile the men hardly breathed as they approached what seemed to be a large herd. As the boat glided forward, Joseph could see several sleek forms swimming around in the water near the floe, and motioned for the men to pull in the oars. The walrus are nearsighted to the point of blindness, but their hearing or feeling in the water is very keen. Everyone lay flat in the boat and the old man made a sign for Jack to do so also. Each oarsman raised up enough to get his outside arm over the side, and they paddled the last quarter mile with their bare hands.

Daddy said he felt that his heart beating against the inside of the bow would alert the whole herd, but Joseph's impassive mask kept everyone in the boat motionless. As one man the men pulled in their arms as the momentum carried the umiak to the edge of the ice.

The old Eskimo chief jabbed once more at his neck to remind Dad of where to aim, and then motioned with his chin for him to stand up and shoot. Dad stood up, raised his rifle, and looked into the face of a huge, drowsy, bull walrus. He could see the half-closed eyelids, and the moisture around the mouth clearly, as the old fellow lay propped up on his side against the ice. As the prow of the boat hit the iceberg, the animal started full awake, and reared up and back. Dad fired directly into the massive neck, and a war exploded in the boat behind him. The Eskimos screamed and laughed as they fired wildly into a herd of about fifteen walrus. Four of them, including Dad's first victim, fell to the ice immediately with broken necks. The natives, still yelling, piled out onto the floe and hurriedly dragged the slight skin boat onto the ice, as the bloody, wounded walrus galloped off into the water. Joseph explained that the big slugs are usually very timid, and will run from any noise or movement, but once they are wounded, they will often attack a boat in the water. The Eskimos were overjoyed at their first kill, and all had to hug each other and shake hands with Jack Palmer in honor of the first shot, as soon as they all turned to and got the umiak up out of the water.

"See, I tell you this white man not so dumb!" bragged Joseph about his friend.

Then the men hacked off the heads of the four walrus and flopped them over into the middle of the boat, leaving the bodies on the ice. The ivory tusk was the most valuable part, and only a small portion of the four- to five-ton animals was used to eat. Besides, Joseph explained, the hunt had only just started, and they had all day to find the choicest animals to butcher for meat.

Apparently they were then on the outer edge of the walrus community, because when they returned to the water, they headed toward the next closest ice floe and found perhaps fifty more walrus. Again there was the hand-paddling, the choking silence, and again the bloody massacre, taking only the tusks.

The third iceberg they approached was like a small island, about five acres across and covered solidly with snoozing walrus. It is possible to see ten miles or more out on the ocean, and the water was strewn thickly with the floe ice, but Daddy said no matter in which direction he looked, or how far, each white patch was black with walrus. The excited natives were terrible shots, but even if they'd worn blindfolds, they could hardly have missed.

Dad kidded old Joseph about this as they waded into the decapitation again, about the waste of meat and how many good animals they only wounded. "No waste, Jack. Cousin, he get 'em up Point Hope, North Cape, Uguluk. Sometime stink pretty bad then, but cousins like 'em. Good to feed dogs, too."

The next floe they approached was quite small, only thirty or forty feet across, but there were plenty of walrus on it to make an attack worthwhile. The Eskimos were very excited, and even more reckless by this time. They killed only two out of twenty or more, but they must have wounded most of the rest, who took to the water. Joseph looked the smallest animal over carefully, and decided this one was worth butchering for meat. So, all hands turned in to carve off the proper hunks after the skin was removed. First they ripped into the belly and removed the kidneys, which weighed about fifteen pounds each. These were tied up with seal gut and immediately hung over the side of the boat into the water to "cook," while the rest of the butchering went on. Then Joseph dived into the stomach cavity again and came up triumphantly with the picnic lunch for the day, enough partially digested clams for all, bits of shell and assorted fish heads included. There are no clams on the beach around Nome, but they must live deep on the bottom where the walrus prowl, because their stomachs are always full of the shellfish.

The next tidbit to be discovered in the huge carcass was a real delicacy, and also considered a sign of very good fortune to the hunt, an unborn baby walrus. Joseph laid it tenderly in one of the seal pokes to take home to feed to the three young brides of the village who hadn't as yet become pregnant.

They were just finishing the butchering when one of the men pointed out at the water. There was a solid ring of walrus approaching the floe, shoulder to shoulder, closing the circle smaller and smaller. The men looked worried and then desperate as the big animals came closer from all sides, only their eyes and tusks showing. Perhaps it was only curiosity, or maybe they were being led by the many pain-crazed walrus who'd been wounded, but Dad could tell that the natives were beginning to get really panicked, that this was something that hadn't happened before.

They all looked, helpless and frozen, at the old leader as Dad said, "What shall we do, Joseph? Shoot 'em?"

"Yeah, shoot 'em," said Joseph weakly, almost as if he were hypnotized by the steadily advancing ring. Then, "Shoot!" he yelled in Eskimo, and everyone with a gun blasted in every direction until the sleek heads disappeared.

Somehow, none of the Eskimos was shot in the attack, and they loaded the last of the boned meat hurriedly into the umiak as if they had been caught stealing in someone else's house. It was time to go home.

By the time the white-blue sky began to dim, they had as much meat as they could carry. The umiak rode very low in the water and the great tusked heads crowded the men at the oars. Everyone was exhausted from the excitement and hard work as they headed for home, so Joseph hauled up the big kidneys for a snack. He bit into one end and knifed off what he needed to chew on, and passed it on to Dad. Daddy borrowed the old man's knife and sliced off a slab to work on, insisting that it was delicious.

Anna had a bright driftwood fire going on the beach while we waited for our men to come home. She had one of her "cousins' " babies on one knee, and me in her lap, as we saw the boat come in.

"See, Ah-leece, I tell you. Waste time to think all the time of bad things!" she laughed. She settled the little ones by the fire, sent the young women off to ready the dinner, and waded out into the ice water with several other grandmas to bring the boat up onto the beach.

CHAPTER 21

However, the ice breaking and *Welcome Spring* were only tantalizing false alarms. There were still long weeks and months to live through until the spring came to Nome. But, just as we all thought we had forgotten the look of sunshine, when it gagged you to smell the cold-storage eggs, and even the beautiful icicles were drizzling and worn out, spring came through. It was time for the first boat, and even our poor little willow tree sent out some feeble shoots. It was wonderful to sink our teeth into a fresh tomato, even if they were twenty- five cents apiece, and Grama sent us a big shipment of home-canned Gravenstein applesauce and wild blackberry jelly and a whole new handmade wardrobe for me.

But every season has to have its disadvantages. In Nome, June brought with it the melting snow, the stinking fish and rotting garbage and sewage of the winter uncovered, and Elva Thorlakkson's clean-up campaign. She never gave up trying to improve Nome and all of us who lived there, and, come June, she really let loose. Of course, the Ladies' Aid was her favored instrument, but she also operated many private crusades.

Millie Bergdorf's saloon was one institution that Elva was out to get, but one day while she was snooping along the beach in back of the place with her binoculars, pretending to look out to sea, Millie caught her focusing on the upstairs windows. In a voice that had once electrified the last row at the Rivoli in Seattle, Millie shouted, "Look out, Elva, who you're pointing those binoculars at. You're likely to find the Reverend himself up here sometime!"

Mrs. Thorlakkson retreated to the guffaws of all Front Street, and that was the end of that scourge for a while, but Elva didn't forget.

Another natural phenomenon in Nome that grated on the Reverend's wife was the Husky dog teams. "In Baltimore, decent people kept dogs in their place! Now I certainly have nothing against pets. Why our little darling Dickie (Dickie was a spindly, homesick canary) is almost as much a member of the family as Precious. But those Huskies . . . well, of course, you might expect it of those filthy Eskimos, the way they have the dogs live right in their shacks with them. But now that sled-racing has become such a popular sport, it isn't safe to walk down Front Street, with a team of those monsters snarling from every yard. Dirty, smelly things—ought to be done away with."

"Now, you can hardly believe this, Mrs. Palmer," she ranted to Mama, "But that—that woman, Millie Bergdorf, has actually trained her whole team to come up here especially to make a toilet of my lovely yard! Well, anyhow, I looked it up at the City Hall, and there's an ordinance that says no dog is allowed on the streets without a leash. And I think it's the duty, the bounden *duty* of every good citizen to see that the law is enforced. I'm going to tell that Sheriff Samson too, and see that he carries through, even if he is a very personal friend of Madam Bergdorf!"

So Elva did tell the Sheriff about the Leashed Dog Ordinance and nagged the good-natured Tagg Samson into admitting it was his duty to enforce the law.

"Sure Elva, you see any loose dogs around, you just come straight to me. I'll put 'em right into the pokey on a good stiff vagrancy charge!"

Tagg may have mentioned the conversation to Millie Bergdorf, but the next morning Elva was stationed behind the glass curtains waiting for the daily call of the fine Carlson dog team. Sure enough, a little before ten o'clock, the nine Huskies boiled out of Millie's yard and headed toward the parish house, each one outfitted with a loosely dangling, new red leash. They didn't know what the joke was about, but they were in a celebrating mood after eating an especially big breakfast and listening to Millie chuckle as she slipped on their new leashes.

They bumbled against one another, and stepped on the dragging leashes as they pranced along like young boys playing hookey. They shouted insults to all the chained dogs along the way, so by the time they approached the Thorlakkson house, Elva was out the door and halfway down the walk to alert the Sheriff.

Just at that moment, Oleson, the lead dog, and Skipper, a nasty half-wolf who'd never learned his place, started to fight. Skipper grabbed the handy red leash and flung Oleson in a half-circle, knocking Mrs. Thorlakkson off her skinny legs, smack into the mud, while Precious squealed from the front porch.

Oleson picked himself up, shook off the mud, and was ready to let bygones be bygones. But not Mrs. Thorlakkson. The war was on! And as with most wars, the most innocent was the first to suffer.

Queenie was the town's loose woman among the dogs. Maybe that was why Elva connected her with Millie Bergdorf and hated her so much, or more likely it was that Millie often took her in and fed the scrawny old vagrant along with her fine team of Huskies. However, Queenie never took on any of Millie's bravado, and no matter how many eggs she fed her, Queenie's coat was still dull and matted. She was very timid and looked embarrassed if anyone spoke to her. She was a small caved-in shepherd of some type, and no one knew when or how she'd ever come to Nome. Queenie had always been there.

Although all the time we knew her, Mama could never reach down to pet her without having her blink and cringe, Queenie loved the children and trusted us without reservation. She was part of all our hide-and-seek, and tag, and tried to please us in complicated games of "house." She even let us dress her in doll hats and wheel her around in the carriage.

It was about a week after Millie Bergdorf's "leashed" dogs had invaded Mrs. Thorlakkson's yard that Mama sent me out to play with Precious and the other children. It was Sunday, shortly after church let out, and most of the town was still drowsing over a second cup of coffee. Mama said she could hear the children's high voices laughing and talking from way down the block. "No, don't shoot her!" shrilled one babyish voice, and she smiled at the funny games that children play. Then she heard a shot, and another one, and once more.

Mama and Daddy were both halfway down the block when they saw me running toward them, my face white and full of agony. I was out of breath and could hardly speak when Mama caught me in her arms and made sure that it wasn't me that was shot.

"Oh Mama, they shot her! Precious was there, and all the kids . . . Mrs. Thorlakkson came running . . . the Sheriff came with a big gun and he shot her . . . but she ran away. She's not dead. Quick Daddy, you can fix her!" I sobbed.

"Great God," said Dad in a pale voice, "Tagg Samson must have shot Elva Thorlakkson! I knew someone would someday!"

When we reached the group of children, they all looked as if they'd been beaten. They held their hands together and looked up at us numbly, while two of the youngest went wailing home. Tagg Samson came around the corner of the Thorlakkson house, his rifle still in his hand.

"Jesus, Jack, that old biddy made me do it. Said it was the law, said she was foaming at the mouth, so I shot her. I shot poor old Queenie! And of course, I didn't kill her, not even with three shots. I always was a lousy shot. She crawled under that old shack next to Thorlakksons' and we can't get under there to finish her off."

Elva came to the door, and by this time quite a crowd had gathered. They could all hear the terrible sounds the dog was making under the house. Elva took Precious' hand and yanked her in the house without a word. No one knew what to say to the children, so we all went home and tried to make lots of noise. But still, everyone in town heard Queenie dying the rest of the afternoon.

CHAPTER 22

Elva Thorlakkson held off for about a month after Queenie died, and Helga Nordstrom was unanimously elected to replace her as President of the Nome Parents and Teachers Association. No one ever talked about the way the little dog died after the first shock wore off, but Elva knew she was out of favor with the town and was determined to redeem her position. So, when Helga graciously named her as First Grade Room Mother for the coming year, Elva found her perfect chance to "do good" again. This time little Maxwell Easiola, the half Eskimo son of the old Negro caretaker at the Golden Gate Hotel, was the victim.

By the time Elva had worked through the old guard of the Ladies' Aid and most of the church choir's quavering old sopranos, the matter of the "poor little youngster's future" was all but settled. Elva's report to the June meeting of the P.T.A. was plainly a mere formality.

She had on her bruise-colored satin crepe and her best church expression that day when she simpered onto the stage. "I'm sure all you ladies are aware of the extremely unfortunate situation of our dear little Maxwell Easiola in regard to the coming school year. Although the child is, uh, approximately eight years old, he has received no formal education or religious training whatever. Of course, the old man takes as good care of him as you would expect of such a person, but I think it is our civic duty to do something really fine for this innocent victim of the unleashed sin which is rampant in our community!" (Polite applause here for rampant sin in community.)

Helga gave Mama the look here, meaning, "See Alice, I told you Elva isn't so bad as you think!"

"Several of the members of the Ladies' Aid have pooled their thoughts on the subject and as Room Mother of the First Grade, I felt called upon to sum up what we've decided." She lowered her blue marble eyes modestly.

"Now then, I happen to know of a simply marvelous mission school down in Seattle run by a lovely, cultured gentleman who was once an associate of the Reverend and myself. Brother Harry Lovering his name is, a fine Christian gentleman who could lead this child in the way that he should go, and Brother Harry has already inquired and found that the Alaska Native Welfare Association will supply ample funds for the boy's tuition there.

"Brother Harry has a settlement house in conjunction with his school, and here the poor little unfortunate orphans have an opportunity to learn the Bible, as well as domestic sciences in the kitchen and laundry work. The children make the most beautiful, touching testimonials about how they've been saved and all; and they also deliver religious literature door to door."

"Now, as President of the Ladies' Aid and active member of this fine organization and First Grade Room Mother, I am willing to take it upon myself to deliver this little waif into the tender care of Brother Harry, personally. Precious and I could take the September boat outside, and the Native Welfare will take . . . ."

"Just one moment, Elva!" Mama bellowed from the back row. "May I ask just why Maxwell cannot be started in our own school here in Nome?"

"Why of course, Alice dear," Elva ruffled back. "Even though you did neglect to be recognized by the chair, I'm delighted to answer any questions and clear up the details before proceeding."

She put on her steel-rimmed glasses and got out a small copy of the Territorial Laws. "In the first place, Ordinance #7668, Section L, Paragraph IV, says that any child of one-half Eskimo blood or more shall be provided for under the Eskimo Welfare Act. In other words, he's half-Eskimo, and although you haven't been in our fair city very long, I'm sure you're aware that the native children do not attend our Nome Elementary and certainly not a little beggar who is part . . . ."

"Just hold on there, Mrs. Thorlakkson," said Mama, trying very hard not to yell. "Isn't it your Sunday School Class that comes home singing so sweetly about 'Jesus loves the little children, all the children of the world. Black and yellow, red and white, they are precious in his sight. Jesus loves the little children of the world!' And besides that, we all know perfectly well that the school has accommodated half-Eskimo children in many cases, especially when the father, acknowledged or not, happened to be one of our more prominent citizens!"

By this time the ladies began to mutter loudly of various protégés, but Elva stopped them short with, "Now girls, I'm sure you all know that I, of all people, would do anything within reason for this dear little child, but after all! After all, Maxwell is no ordinary half-Eskimo. He's half Negro! How would you like your little girls sharing a desk with this little pickaninny? You Mrs. Palmer, " she added in a trembling voice, "how would you like your little Artis *married* to Maxwell?"

"Well actually, Elva, I think five years old is a little young for Artis to be thinking about marrying even the blondest Swede in the whole first grade!"

The laughter was more than Elva could stand. She brought out her ace in the hole. "Very well, then. I didn't want to mention this, but sarcasm forces me to bring out the real seriousness of the situation, " she said, wetting her thin lips eagerly. "Maxwell Easiola is a . . . Well, I mean he's not uh, legitimate! Of course, everyone knows how Joe and that Lena Ikiyuna were living there together. Her and her whole passel of the other brats moved in bag and baggage. You could hear them all plain as day if you walked by close to the old Golden Gate, laughing and singing in there just as if everything was all open and above board. Why, I even happened to glance in the back window one day and there she was, nursing the last one, big as life, and he had his arm around her, *watching!*"

At this Helga stood up and said hurriedly, "Well, thank you very much, Mrs. Thorlakkson, for your study of . . . ."

"You're very welcome, I'm sure, Mrs. Nordstrom, but I do want to stress this last point for Mrs. Palmer and some of the others like that. And that is, that Maxwell Easiola is certainly not entitled to come to school next fall with Precious and all the rest. He's a half-Eskimo, half Negro at that, he's illegitimate, and not even baptized."

But by this time the Parents and Teachers Association had turned into a very loud and free discussion of the whole problem, each lady trying to outshout the other.

Helga finally climbed up on her chair and banged the gavel until its head was ready to fly off. "Meeting adjourned!" she shouted. "Thank you all, ladies, for your interest. We'll continue this discussion at the next meeting!"

And continue the discussion they did, all the way out of the meeting, down the steps, and down the streets to their houses, gabbling and shrilling, shaking heads and waving hands. They all told their husbands what opinions they should take, and by dinnertime that evening, probably everyone in Nome except Maxwell and Joe Easiola knew the whole story and had taken sides.

Daddy was horrified at Elva's plan for the little boy. "Somebody ought to put that biddy in a nice padded cell where she could get her kicks out of sticking pins in rag dolls. I can just see that fine mission school in Seattle! Probably one of those deals where a bunch of religious fanatics send the little kids around to the door selling their phony magazines. And the thing about it is that the boy is really smart. Remember I told you about talking to him when we first came up here last summer? Joe and the kid sit for hours paging through the old *National Geographic's*, and talking about the different places. Kurt and I took him up with us for a couple of days at the camp, and Kurt says he's a natural mechanic too. He probably takes care of the old man, rather than the other way around."

"I know, Jack, and I feel sick about it," said Mama. "The trouble is, it's our own fault. We should have seen to it that Maxwell started school last fall. Then Elva never would have thought of him for her crusade."

Helga dropped in as soon as she got Janet to sleep, and joined the discussion. "Now Alice, what are we going to do about the little boy? I feel we *must* help him out of this. Even if he was only sent to the Mission School for Eskimos on King Island, I think the old man's heart would break. The boy is all he has, you know, and I think I would never be able to face myself again if the little fellow is shipped off away from his father!"

Helga looked as if she might cry, so Mama settled her with some black coffee and *Klumpsukkerr*. "Now Helga, you can't take this so hard. After all, just because you're the P.T.A. president, you can't take a personal responsibility for each child. Besides, we'll think of something."

Mama was just refilling Helga's cup, when we saw Millie Bergdorf coming up the front steps.

"Hello, Millie. Come on in," said Mama. "You must have smelled the coffee!"

"Hello, Mrs. Palmer, Jack. How do you do Mrs. Nordstrom? I'm glad to find you all still up. I won't stay long, but I wanted to talk to you about the boy down at the hotel. Tagg Samson was telling me about my friend Elva's plans for him."

Mama handed Millie a cup of coffee, and as Millie poured in canned milk and lit a cigarette, Helga noticed that her hands were clean and well kept; so were her clothes and hair. Her manner was relaxed and pleasant, and Helga decided that she liked Millie, even if she did run a saloon.

"I've got what you might call a reference on this Brother Harry of hers," Millie chuckled. "Harry Sampsle, his name was then, back in 1918 in Seattle. We were both in the same business, so to speak, but he only sold *pictures* of girls—usually through the carnivals and dime-a-dance spots. But he got a little too greedy for his own good, and tried cheating the cops he had to pay to lay off him. Brother Harry ended up doing a couple of years in

Walla Walla for sending his stuff through the mails. Then when he got out he started this new racket, religion. They say he's been making a killing ever since. The mission part takes care of fleecing the lonesome old suckers, and then on the side he runs this school deal to do the kitchen work and 'spread the word.' Anyway, I thought you might be able to use it for what it's worth. Maxwell has been in the tavern a few times to cadge a meal, and I always liked the little guy."

"Poor Elva. I'm sure she couldn't have known this," said Helga sincerely. "But the trouble is, Millie, if she gives up on Brother Harry, she's bound to take Maxwell to some other place. Come on, Millie, pull your chair up to the table here. Four heads are better than three. I got a copy of the Territorial Laws down at the City Hall this afternoon, and I'm sure we can figure something out," said Mama.

Dad, Helga, Millie, and Mama struggled in and out of the complicated legal phrases until they were all dizzy, but the trouble was that legally Maxwell just did not exist. Of course, there had been no physician or other person attendant at his birth. So there was no birth certificate for him, and not even a witness to swear that he was born, let alone to say who his father and mother were and what their race. Joe Easiola owned no property and paid no taxes, so he was just a ghost, too. Most of the time he lived in the happy days of the gold rush, and if he and Maxwell needed anything he usually begged it from some of the other old-timers.

"Well dammit," grumbled Millie, "why don't you just take the kid up to school when you take your girl next fall and enroll him. Nobody is going to hold it against an eight-year-old boy just because they aren't sure of who his mother is. Why, hell, I can think of lots of old guys in this town who aren't too sure of their old man!"

"But the trouble is, Millie," complained Helga, "the School Board members are the ones who would decide whether to let him in or not, and you know who they are. Elva Thorlakkson, Reverend Thorlakkson, Jim Swenson, the undertaker (his wife is

Elva's dearest buddy), and Jake Welty and Dr. Jenner. I think the Doctor and Welty would be all right, but . . . ."

"Baloney," interrupted Millie, "you're sure the optimist if you think Jake Welty would give him a break, Alice. That old buzzard has no use for Eskimos."

"Well, they have the majority no matter which way you count it. Elva must have been working on this for quite a while before she brought it out at the meeting. They'll never let Maxwell in Nome Elementary." Mama filled the coffee cups again. "Even if we could prove Lena Ikiyuna is his mother, then that would establish him as half Eskimo, and he could attend the King Island School. Poor baby. He's just like Peter Pan. If only he had a mother!"

"Just a minute, boys and girls!" crowed Millie. "I'm having myself a brainstorm! And why it took me all this time to figure out something so sweet and simple, I'll never know! *I'll* be Maxwell's mother!"

"You mean you'd adopt the . . . ."

"Oh no, Alice, that'd be too slow—probably take months. No, I'll be his real natural-born mother. I always did want to try my hand at raising something besides Siberian Huskies, but I was always making too much money to quit. Maxwell's a little dark, of course, but hell, who cares?"

"Don't you see how perfect it'll work?" she said excitedly. "I was right here in Nome the winter before Maxwell was born, and that summer I went outside for about three months. No one met me at the boat when I came back. Why, I could have had triplets with me and no one would have noticed. And old Joe used to amble down to my place now and then for a free drink. Still does, in fact. No one saw much of Maxwell till he was a couple of years old, and began to toddle around."

"There would still be no proof," protested Helga.

"But that's where you're wrong, honey. The old nurse at the hospital, Tilly Eckmann, and I have been friends for years here in Nome. She spent the summer of 'twenty-seven down South too. Fairbanks, I think it was, but it don't make no difference. There's our midwife and A Number One witness, and I'm sure Tagg Samson can get us the birth certificate form from Fairbanks with all necessary dates and stuff fixed in. His brother-in-law practically runs Fairbanks. Why, I tell you, kids, it's a perfect setup."

"Millie, I can't tell you what a fine thing this is for you to do," beamed Helga. "But are you sure this is what you want? Think what the ladies will say."

"Heck, don't give them a thought, Helga. I never do. I haven't exactly been on the Nome Social Register for quite some time now anyway, but I never let that get me down. Hell, 'Rise above it Millie,' I tell myself. Besides, I always liked that cute little tike. In fact, I think I *love* him! By God, and why not? He's my own son, isn't he?"

Millie laughed and winked broadly as she rose. "Now give Tagg and Tilly and me a few days or maybe a week. Fritz Niemyer makes an airplane trip to Fairbanks on Tuesday and he can be back with the papers by Friday. Then I'll get the word to you and you can let Elva have the terrible 'truth' right away."

A week later when Helga went calling on the minister's wife, Elva was delighted to discuss further her favorite crusade. "Yes, Mrs. Thorlakkson, that's why I came. Sometimes there are things that just can't be discussed at a public meeting, and I know that I can depend on you to keep a secret," said Helga.

"Of course, dear. You know my lips are sealed." Elva flew to put on the coffee and lay out the Fig Newtons.

"This has been a very well-guarded secret, Mrs. Thorlakkson, and I'd never mention it to anyone but you, because of your kind interest in the boy, and then too, I'm sure you would never want to hurt another woman's reputation here in town!"

Elva insisted on another Fig Newton for Helga, and drew her chair closer.

"Well, you see, Tagg Samson heard about the goings-on at P.T.A. last week and started to do a little checking on his own. He wrote air mail down to the Bureau of Records in Fairbanks, and sure enough there *was* a birth certificate for Maxwell Easiola and . . . now mind you, not a word of this to anyone. The mother is listed as Mildred Marie Bergdorf! Of Nome, Alaska!"

Elva sat back, part of a Fig Newton still unchewed in her open mouth. "No!" was all she could manage. Then, "No, I can't believe it!" she squealed delightedly.

"Now, I know this will never be passed on in any way by you, Mrs. Thorlakkson, but I wanted you to know so you wouldn't go to any more trouble on the mission school in Seattle, and so forth."

"Well, Helga dear, it was no trouble at all. I get a great deal of satisfaction out of helping our more unfortunate ones. But of course if he isn't part Eskimo, well then. . . . but I know you must be busy now with all your P.T.A. duties, so I won't keep you."

Helga said Elva practically poured the coffee down her neck, getting her hat and coat back on, in the rush to get her out and be on her way to tell the "girls." It must have been a great disappointment to give up the saving of Maxwell and his trip to Brother Harry, but she probably felt more than rewarded for the loss of the trip by the opportunity of telling everyone she could get hold of about Millie Bergdorf's ghastly crime.

Anyone with good sense realized that putting the fair skinned, red-headed, pale-eyed Millie Bergdorf over as Maxwell's mother was a great joke on Elva Thorlakkson. But then, Elva's clique was not noted for their common sense. In fact, everyone in town said that Elva herself must have known that the dark, almond-eyed little boy couldn't have been Millie's son, but she was having too much fun slandering her to stop and think.

So Maxwell started Nome Elementary that fall and was soon promoted to second grade. One of the smartest boys in the class, they said.

CHAPTER 23

Edgar St. George and Kurt and Daddy had been commuting by tractor back and forth between Nome and Cripple Creek since mid-April, getting the dredge and other mining equipment in working order. The three men were living in a tent on the dredge as a temporary arrangement, while they waited for the creek to thaw and for the snow to melt off the tundra so they could start mining.

Kurt again was in charge of the antique dredge. The old-fashioned one-cylinder gasoline engine had been made in 1903 in San Francisco, so of course replacement parts were out of the question. Instead, he made his own parts out of ingenuity, Swedish cussing, and thirty-year-old junk found in and around Nome. Daddy said Kurt did everything but make love to the old wreck, but by June the huge fly wheel was whizzing, and the twenty large cast-iron buckets were clanking around on their endless chain, ready to start chewing into the river bed.

After considerable difficulty, St. George found the spot on the creek where they had left off digging the summer before. His first task was to try to figure which way the vein of gold was coming from, so they would know where to start the dredge digging. The men would pour buckets of boiling water down into his many prospecting holes along the water's edge to keep the ice thawed. Then Edgar would dig down to the dirt, fill his shallow pan with the slush ice and gravel, and swirl it around with more hot water until the gold (if any) sank to the bottom of the pan. Of course, every bucket of water had to be heated on the big wood-burning stove, and every stick of wood had to be hauled from Nome, so Daddy was busy, too.

His job was to scour the town and surrounding mines out on the tundra for old machine parts that might be usable for the dredge, and to keep the camp supplied with food and firewood from Nome. Quite by accident, he had stumbled across another old half-sunken barge several miles further out on the creek. After almost half a day's snow-shoveling, they discovered a real treasure trove of hand-forged dredge parts, all still packed in their wooden cases. Kurt fell on them as if they were diamonds, and after a minor cleaning and sorting job, they were as good as new. Even after thirty years of winters on the tundra, the dry, frozen snow had preserved the machinery as perfectly as if it had been on the warehouse shelves.

Also, Count Barkavitch was back in town and had established his spring camp in the cozy lobby of the hotel, so Dad was the go-between for all the threats and abuse and ridiculous instructions from the Count to poor St. George. He had the answer to every problem of the camp, from exactly where the gold lay under the earth to how much baking powder it took to make biscuits rise.

By the end of May, the whole tundra was oozing with melted snow and half-frozen mud. Every puddle was a breeding place for billions of mosquitoes, but the men didn't even take time out to swat them away. The teakettle on the stove was still frozen stiff every morning, but St. George hoped to start two twelve-hour shifts of men working by June 15. Then, if the weather co-operated, they would have about one hundred days to work before the snow came again in September. Even the water in the creek was in a hurry as it chuckled along its banks down toward the sea.

However, St. George and the Count soon found there was a very serious hitch in recruiting men in Nome for the summer's work. Before they even asked about wages, they all wanted to know who was going to be the cook for the camp. Florence Beck was by that time a happily married town lady, and Gust was working for Wagner Commercial Company, so the Snake River Exploratory Corporation had a real personnel problem.

Several women were mentioned, but for one reason or another, all were ruled out. Sis Nelson was addicted to drinking before breakfast, Mrs. Sposari was known to be so cranky that she turned the milk sour, and Angie Cronkhite was inclined to multiple love affairs among the miners. Someone even thought of old Joe Easiola, but they said he always wandered off to pick wild flowers and got lost.

It was Kurt Nordstrom who finally came up with the idea of having Helga as the "bull-cook." Helga wasn't at all keen about the plan of spending the summer out on the tundra cooking for two shifts of hungry men, until she thought of having Mama and me come along.

"Alice and I could spell each other on meals," she suggested. "And besides, Artis and Janet would have such a wonderful time!"

The Count grumbled for a while about extra mouths to feed and the terrors of children being ground into the gears of the machinery, but hunger prevailed. By June 15, our jeans and sweaters and heavy shoes and boots were packed in among the food cartons for the first trip to camp. Daddy piled us all in on top of old iron wagon wheels and oil drums and strange-looking rusted machinery in the big rubber-tired wagon in back of the tractor. Janet and I perched on the very top of the load as we rumbled through Nome down the main street to the beach, with every kid in town waving and squealing and wishing they could go along.

By this time Dad had discovered that the smoothest way to ride was right along the water line on the beach, rather than cross-country on the tundra. After about two hours' ride along the hard-packed sand, we came to the flat mud delta of Cripple Creek where it entered the ocean. There had been a heavy rainstorm two days earlier, so Dad's tracks from his former trips had washed away. However, he'd been careful to line up landmarks and was certain of where the sandbar was that led up through the center of the river. He aimed the little tractor straight up the swollen creek at full speed to keep from getting stuck on the bottom. Janet and I dangled our feet over the side of the clumsy wagon, delighted at the sight of the water rushing by on either side, when suddenly the tractor disappeared into the river, and Daddy was in water up to his armpits.

Mama thought he'd lost his mind when he dove into the water and unshackled the wagon from the tractor. We immediately started rolling backward down toward the ocean until he caught up with us and shoved the loaded wagon, wives, kids, pots and pans over to the bank of the creek.

Daddy was so mad he couldn't even swear. Janet and I had enough sense to shut up, for once, and sit still until they decided what to do. The little cat, still bubbling, lay in about ten feet of water, where the firm sandbar had formerly been, and we were still half a day's ride from the camp upstream.

After rejecting Dad's suggestion that we all march down to the Bering Sea and drown ourselves, Helga and Mama started sorting through the suitcases and came up with a complete dry outfit for him, including a pair of Kurt's new boots, size fourteen. Somehow, the matches were still dry, and by the time Daddy started hiking toward camp for help, Mama had a small bonfire going near the wagon.

He was still so mad at the river changing the course of its once trusty sandbank, that he must have run all the way to camp. By the time Mama and Helga had the squad tent set up and a sketchy meal started, all the men of the camp came splashing down the river toward us. Everyone was loaded with chains and ropes and shovels and picks and bad ideas how to get the cat out of the water, and even worse jokes on how it had gotten in.

By dark, all the men were fed, the dishes rinsed in the river, and all fourteen of us wedged ourselves into the tent. The women spread several oilcloth table covers on the ground, and then all our blankets over this. Everyone lay down fully dressed, shoes, hats and all, and soon there was a chorus of ten exhausted snoring men that worked like a lullaby. St. George, the Nordstroms, the Palmers, three of the Blue Fox's worst drunks, three half-Eskimos, and another man named Jim, whose last name we never did learn, all snuggled together and slept like lambs.

Although Janet and I thought it was as much fun as a picnic, we wasted three days of our precious hundred in pulling the little cat out of the river. The men tried all kinds of fancy schemes to haul it out with chains and block and tackle, but eventually it came down to simple manpower. Each one took his turn diving down into the ice water, holding his breath till he felt like exploding, and turning the manual crank at the front of the cat, which turned the cleats an inch at a time. Then he'd pop up to the surface again, and thaw out at the fire until it was his turn to dive again. After about twelve hours of this, they got the cat far enough up onto the sand so they could pull it with chains from either side of the river.

"Just like the Volga boatmen, eh boys?" said St. George. "Thank God the Count isn't with us!"

Then Kurt completely dismantled the whole tractor and the women dried out every part, every screw, in pans over the fire. By the end of the third day, Kurt and St. George wrenched the last nut and bolt back together and to everyone's amazement, it started. We arrived at the Snake River Exploratory Corporation Summer Camp about three hours later to cheers from all hands.

The men had been living on canned beans for about a week before we arrived and you would have thought it was Mae West and Jean Harlow coming to camp for all the fuss they made. The skinny old man named Jim said, "If it was just Jack and that tractor, we would have left him down on the bottom of Cripple Creek till September. But for such a beautiful bunch of ladies, cooks to boot, well I guess we would have dived right down to the floor of the Bering Sea to fish 'em out!"

Also, several precious days had been spent in moving in an old shack Daddy had found several miles upstream from the camp. The way they had been raving over the luxury of living in a real house, we were expecting something on the order of Monticello. Actually it was more like a huge, two-story doghouse, only much dirtier. Some Eskimos must have made it their summer camp for a few seasons by the looks of the mounds of old fish heads thrown in the comers, and several families of ground squirrels still occupied the upstairs rooms.

So Mama and Helga insisted on setting up the squad tent again as a cook shack until the house was cleaned. Old Jim carried the nests of baby squirrels out onto the tundra in his hat as tenderly as a mother cat with kittens. And then the cleaning crew moved in. Mama and Helga both wore rubber hip boots and dish towels over their heads, but the place was so disgustingly dirty they didn't know where to start. It was Jim who thought of bringing in one of the big fire hoses from the creek, and this worked fine. Janet and I got into our boots too and sloshed around in the Fels Naphtha suds to our hearts' delight. Jim got a little too enthusiastic with the final rinse and loosened the boards around the doors and windows so badly that you could see daylight through in quite a few places, but at least it was clean.

The men moved in the old stove from the Golden Gate Hotel that they had used the summer before, and also nailed up the wooden packing-cases that the food had come in for cupboards. An oil drum cut in half was the kitchen sink, but most of the dishwashing was done in the creek. The creek also served as a community bath tub, and a pleasant one at that. Daddy had dredged out a shallow pool close to the cabin, and the almost continual sunshine kept the water quite warm for swimming.

Once summer finally comes to the tundra, it comes in a rush. From the end of June, the sun hardly sets at all, and the days are long and warm. The sun came up very early in the morning, circled around the dome of the sky, and then set very late at night in almost the same spot where it had come up. This made it impossible to establish directions on the tundra unless you knew landmarks, and of course, time of day became rather theoretical too. It was almost always light and sunny and warm, so life went according to what shift was working and when meals were served.

The two cooks soon found that men who worked twelve hours at a stretch needed more than three meals. At 7 A.M. they fixed a huge meal for everyone in camp which served as breakfast for the men starting to work, and dinner for those who had worked through the night. This included meat, potatoes, eggs, pancakes, fruit, and dessert. Then around ten, there was a coffee break for the day shift, with more cake or pie. At noon, Janet and I felt very important to be able to carry great sacks of sandwiches and coffee and dessert out to the dredge for lunch. If it was hot, the men ate again about three, usually a salad and cold juice or iced tea. Then the big meal of the day was served at seven. We usually dined on whatever fresh meat Dad was able to bring in—ptarmigan or reindeer, fresh salmon or trout from the creek—along with potatoes, homemade bread, coffee, and more dessert. Then while Mama cleaned up the dishes and got us ready for bed, Helga laid out the midnight lunch for the second shift.

But even with all this cooking to be done, there was still time to have fun at camp that summer. None of us had thought of bringing bathing suits to the Arctic Circle, so Helga and Mama fixed themselves bathing suits made out of old worn-out union suits cut off at the arms and legs. As for Janet and me, we swam naked as a couple of trout. Our only audience was a pretty red fox and her two curious cubs. Each day, as they got used to the noise and bustle of camp, the fox family grew bolder. Finally, even the big fox would come right up to the steps of the shack to beg for scraps, and the two youngsters would have moved right into our sleeping bags if we could have smuggled them past the kitchen. Also we could wander for miles over the tundra and still be within sight of camp, so we often were allowed to go berry-picking or mushroom-gathering by ourselves. One day Anna and Joseph Aloruk came up from their summer fishing camp and took Janet and me into the foothills to gather Arctic tern eggs. The perfect days flew by too fast.

By July the tundra was overflowing with beauty, as well as delicacies to eat. Wild honeysuckle twined itself around the blueberry bushes which were glutted with fruit. The ptarmigan were so thick they had to be shoved away to get at the endless acres of mushrooms. The creek was full of trout, and hundreds of thousands of ducks and geese flew over camp every morning and evening. Reindeer herds grazed past in the mountains back of camp every few days, and great ten-pound Arctic hares went into the stewpot two or three times every week. The sun shone, and the sweet flowers bloomed and the game practically fell into our laps. The whole tundra was as lavish as a splendid tapestry, with everything a man could want. Everything except gold.

Actually gold-mining is nothing more than washing dirt. Either by science or witchcraft or old wives' tales or divining rods or willow wands, you choose your place to dig. Then by pick and shovel or $100,000 dredge you dig out your chosen dirt and run it through water. Then you channel it down a long trough called a sluice box with crossbars on it to catch the gold. In these little crossbars, called riffles, you place quicksilver, and then wait for the tiny gold nuggets and flakes to collect.

All summer long the men labored to wash the dirt. Thousands of cubic yards of it stacked up into mountains in back of the camp. Mountains of nice, clean, washed dirt-but still no gold. The rich vein from the summer before had simply ended. As the breezes began to take on a slightly minty coolness, the men worked like slaves, never stopping even on Sundays to catch their breath. But they couldn't seem to find the pay dirt. Even Mama and Helga helped with the furious panning to try to figure in which direction the gold had headed. Then when St. George found a sample of gravel that had a promising percentage of gold in it, all hands would turn out to set up the dredge in the right direction. Kurt would get the cranky old machinery set to dig into the river bed at the new spot. Then St. George carefully filled the riffles of the sluice with quicksilver to catch the gold as the dirt and water and gravel passed down the funnel. They would dig until the iron buckets bit shudderingly into solid rock, called bedrock, with nothing but a tantalizing flouring of gold showing in the riffles.

As September approached all the men worked as if they were possessed, but Kurt Nordstrom was the worst. He had been bitten by the gold bug, and couldn't stop even long enough to eat and sleep. He'd bolt down his dinner and then gallop back out to the dredge to dig, halfway into the night, with the second shift. Each rock that got stuck in the buckets was a personal enemy, and every day that went by without their finding gold was a deep insult. Helga was afraid he was going to make himself sick, and then to make matters even worse, the Count moved out to camp.

He thundered around blowing cigar smoke in everyone's eyes, telling the men what they were doing wrong and even accused Kurt of finding gold secretly and digging it for himself at night. The usually good-tempered St. George looked as if he were about to have a stroke by the time old Jim finally "accidentally" dropped a chunk of granite the size of a watermelon on the Count's instep, and he fled back to Nome.

By the first of September, defeat lay over the camp like something palpable. The wind off the Bering Sea whistled through the holes in the walls of the shack and left a fine frost on our hair when we woke up in the morning. The men had to wear gloves to work in, but then they would get wet and freeze solid on their hands. Finally one morning the pond was too frozen to even get wash water for the dishes, and the cooks rebelled and demanded to be taken home. Kurt was sure he could *smell* the gold, it was so close, but when he had to start the dredge engine by thawing it with a blowtorch, even St. George gave up. He and Dad and Kurt stayed behind to close up the camp for the winter, but Jim took the rest of the crew and Helga and Janet and Mama and me back in the wagon to Nome.

A few days later the men brought the season's take into town. The Count carried the can of gold dust and nuggets to the bank, and watched like an eagle as Jake Welty weighed it out on the scale. By the time he had paid wages of about twelve dollars a day to Kurt and Dad and the other seven men, there was precious little left for the Snake River Exploratory Corporation. At St. George's insistence, the Count also peeled off three dollars a day for both Helga and Mama for their summer's work.

"It almost made me ashamed to take the money, the way he looked when he paid us," said Mama. "You would have thought he was pulling his fingernails right off along with the dollar bills.

But when we figured it out, Helga and I worked like dogs that whole summer long for what amounted to about twenty-five cents an hour!"

As the Palmers and the Nordstroms left the bank lobby, wise old Jake, the banker, called them over to his desk. He stood and put his arms around Dad and Kurt in a fatherly way and said, "If you boys managed to make wages for the summer and got cured of the gold bug at the same time, you just learned one of the cheapest lessons you're likely to get. Find yourselves a good, honest job peddlin' shoelaces and you'll be better off in the long run than chasin' your lives away lookin' for gold!"

CHAPTER 24

That fall Mama, Daddy, and I stood with the rest of the winter people to see the last boat leave Nome. From all the letters from home, there seemed to be no good reason for going back to Seattle. Uncle Max wrote that Grama's leg had healed better than anyone had hoped it would. In fact, she never did get around to making the patchwork quilt she had planned to do while she was in the cast. At seventy, she decided the quilt could wait until she got to be an old lady. Instead, she'd put in a large corn patch that spring and made such a good crop that she'd been able to take most of it down to the Salvation Army Home for Old Men. Max also wrote us that times were still very bad, especially in the building trades. So the Palmers decided to stay another winter in Nome. Besides, like many another sourdough, we didn't have the money for the fare home.

With the rest of the regulars, we waved good-by to the ones who were going "outside." As the *Victoria* belched one final blast, Jimmy Roach nudged Mama. "There they go, the lucky stiffs. I could stand me a nice winter on the beach down in California right now. And how about you, Alice?"

"Oh, I don't know, Jimmy. I actually kind of like Nome in the winter, once the snow comes to cover up all the dirt and smell," said Mama, smiling.

"Whoops boys, there she goes!" he cackled to a few of his cronies. "That's how all the old sourdoughs talk at first. Next thing she'll be seeing her wolf-fur mitts dancing and barking around the cabin floor, and telling us the northern lights spelled out her name in the sky. That's what comes of missing too many boats!"

The old men loved to joke each other about being sourdoughs, but there was really a knack to living out the Nome winter. The four to five hundred people that were left moved closer together and settled down to wait. Once the last boat left and the cold locked us in, there was nothing left but to get along with your fellow human beings as comfortably as possible.

There was a new show (new to Nome, that is) every week, or you could listen to the static on the earphones down at the radio station, or you could get drunk at the Blue Fox or Millie Bergdorf's. But this was the time when most folks got together to develop the fine, almost lost art of conversation. There wasn't even a sunrise to divide the winter nights from the dark days, and many times only the eight o'clock alarm could break up the talk. With six empty, dark months to fill, one whole night didn't seem too long to talk over the Townsend Plan, what was between Hearst and that Davies woman, whether prohibition could last, if there was a God, or whether Will Rogers would make a good President.

Coffee and cake were always an important part of the talk, too. The first few months, when the eggs were still fairly fresh, the women would turn out the Lady Baltimore cakes—three perfect white, puffy layers, filled with chopped nuts mixed in goo of figs and candied cherries, frosted with Seven-Minute Special in stiff white peaks. As the eggs got riper, they switched to feather devil's food with mocha chocolate frosting, or Mrs. Wagner's favorite spice cake with maple crush topping. Of course, the coffee pot was always kept warm on the back of the stove, and there was usually someone visiting, ready to drink it and have "just a sliver" of cake.

And of course, there was always a party going on somewhere in town. We had bridge parties and baby showers, birthday parties and wedding anniversaries, P.T.A. meeting, socials, and dances. And every one of them required dressing to the hilt. Even the simplest afternoon bridge game with the girls called for silk stockings, high heels, an afternoon dress, hat, gloves, and purse. Then, even if the game was only next door, over all this finery had to go wool ski pants, a heavy sweater, fur parka and hood, heavy mitts, and mukluks. As a matter of course, when you arrived at a party the first step was to adjourn to the nearest bedroom to take off mukluks, parka and ski pants and put on your inside hat, gloves, and shoes for your formal entrance.

But when the mothballs really flew in Nome was for the town's many formal functions. The International Order of Odd Fellows gave a ball every winter, so the Ladies of The Eastern Star had to go them one better and give two dances during the social season. Then there was always a New Year's Eve party at the Hotel, the Nome Sweepstakes Ball, and a great celebration after the election of local officials every September.

This victory dance (or dirge of defeat, depending on who you voted for) was usually one of the highlights of the winter. By then the last boat had gone, school had started for the kids, and the Nome regulars had commenced the serious business of wintering in earnest.

Since most folks only went "outside" once every four or five years, and didn't have much money to spend when they did, the party dresses for these social occasions were little wonders. Some took the easy way and ordered from the Sears catalogue and hoped for the best. Others tried making their own, usually with the results turning out to look pretty seamy. Those who had given up trying to impress anyone of anything had one or two old stand-bys that they wore grimly to all parties, no matter how many there were.

Helga Nordstrom had the good black lace she had bought in Los Angeles in 1921 when styles were very short. However, with the rhinestone tiara she had won on the boat coming up to lead the eyes away from her sturdy, bare knees, she felt quite stylish.

Mama had taken Aunt Lilly's advice and packed two great slinky evening gowns; one tangerine crepe trimmed with dangling beads that wiggled when she walked, and one beautiful emerald chiffon and lace with a dippy handkerchief hemline. This made the decision of what to wear beautifully simple. The green did nicely for anything requiring dignity and restraint, and the orange beaded job for all the rest. The emerald chiffon was hardly worn, but the jazzy orange crepe went everywhere.

Of course, the Victory Ball after Tagg Samson was reelected Sheriff that fall was anything but dignified, so Mama shimmered forth in the beaded crepe, her hair fluffed out in a terrible Nome permanent, and ready for anything. Tagg had been the Sheriff for twenty years, so Millie Bergdorf and all the Blue Fox gang were there. But in that same election, Reverend Thorlakkson squeaked in as city councilman, so the reform movement was also at the ball in force. In fact, everyone in town who could walk was at the dance, even the kids. There was no one left at home to baby-sit, so the I.O.O.F. wives fixed up a room in the basement of the hall for us. We were supposed to stay down there, but no one wanted to be stuck with the guard duty, so we saw quite a bit of the Victory Ball, too.

The orchestra that night was Jimmy Roach and his violin, somebody playing the snare drums, and Millie Bergdorf at the piano. Jimmy wore his usual costume of wool shirt and pants and Eskimo fur slippers, but the drummer appeared in a venerable old tuxedo, black tie, and mukluks. Millie slithered up onto the platform in a long red dress covered solidly with red sequins, only slightly tarnished, and a red feather boa that must have seen service on the stage in one of her many interesting former careers.

With both the well-entrenched regulars and the new reform party represented, politics made some very strange dancing partners that night. The orchestra started off with a polka and a couple of schottisches just to warm things up, and every Swede in town swung onto the floor—Kurt and Helga, Gust and Florence, and all the rest. Even Nome's several grandmas hopped around in tune to the lively music, often with men young enough to be their grandsons.

Jimmy Roach held up on the fiddle as long as he could stand the thirst, but finally threw it down and bolted for the bar. He could never stand to see anyone else mix drinks, and soon he was fixing everyone with potent, old-fashioned concoctions that had been forgotten thirty years before. Then after a few stiff straight shots for himself, he set out to dance with every lady at the

Victory Ball. He went right down the line, from young matrons with babies on their laps to sour- puss old ladies with shaky legs. All had their turn with Jimmy.

He fitted under Mama's arm perfectly, and she said it was like dancing with a leprechaun, the way he hopped about, laughing fit to kill, the whole time. No one knows what he said to make all the other women blush and smile, but with Mama it was the tangerine crepe that caught his eyes.

"Ah, young Alice, how I would love to have a fine-lookin' woman like you on my arm for a stroll down O'Connell Street. The broadest street in the world, you know! And in just that very frock with the beads all a jigglin' like they do!"

As for the gold-miners, they made every lady feel like a belle. They all spent the summer months alone out on the tundra looking for gold, and their long dark winters were not too much more sociable. So when they came to a dance, they weren't fussy about what songs were played or the menu for the midnight supper. The miners came to dance, and the closer the better. From Millie Bergdorf's barn-silo figure to Elva's sweetheart neckline and puff sleeves, all the girls looked good to them. Leaky Pete always chose Tessie Welty, the banker's stylish wife, for all the fast numbers, because he said, "She's so dang nice and fat, a guy can really get a hold on her!"

One song that all three of the musicians happened to know was "Tales of the Vienna Woods." Count Barkavitch must have known somehow that Elva Thorlakkson was the only lady in the house who had been to dancing school. So before her shadowy husband had time to object, the magnificent old man swept Elva to the dance floor for the waltz. After one mad swing around the room, even the minister must have known he had lost his helpmate for the evening.

The Count danced as if he were in the throes of some sort of religious experience. His beard whipped back over his shoulders and he was likely to shout on the fancy turns. But most incredible to everyone, Elva followed him like a veritable Pavlova. She had the look of someone who has been nibbling at the sacred mushrooms and sees things unseen by others. Her plump feet tripped over the waxed boards faster than light, and her pale pink taffeta-covered bosom swelled with excitement.

Elva and the Count danced every dance that night, and Mrs. Thorlakkson didn't really come back to herself until the Reverend claimed her for the last dance. Then, as she tried to settle her snail-shell curls back into their regular order and pulled her corset back down where it belonged, the old Count joined the other gentlemen at the bar.

"Poor Elva," said Mama. "The lost look on her face as she and the little preacher minced around the floor to 'Goodnight Ladies' was enough to break your heart. I guess it's the only time I ever really liked her."

At the midnight intermission, supper was served, and only just in time. Several of the gold-miners had to be held down and force-fed, but eventually the hot coffee and good food did its work. Daddy and Kurt and Edgar St. George were the bouncers that evening, but they didn't have to subdue anyone and there was only one fist-fight out on the steps.

Tagg Samson was a good hunter and, with several of his deputies, had furnished enough cold roast ptarmigan for everyone. The Ladies' Aid brought the salads and fresh rolls, and the Past Worthy Matrons of the Eastern Star furnished cake and coffee for dessert. Everyone carried their food to the long picnic boards and benches which seated twenty at a time. In the stampede to fill plates and find chairs, an odd assortment of people sat across from each other. Father Murphy and Millie Bergdorf, the Ladies' Aid Executive Council and the Blue Fox bunch all sat down and broke their bread, and exchanged views on what should be done about the wooden sidewalks caving in on Front Street, and whether solitary contemplation did much good to help out the moral problems of the world. Nobody was known to have changed his mind, but on the other hand, no blood was shed either.

With the combination of very short after-dinner speeches and very tall after-dinner drinks, the whole affair soon degenerated into group singing. Millie and Jimmie and the drummer took us through "Long, Long Trail A'Winding" and "Harvest Moon" and "My Wild Irish Rose" and all the rest of the good old songs, till there wasn't a dry eye in the house.

Jimmy Roach was reminded of the past dances that were held in the good old days when Nome was wide-open, anything goes, rip-snorter of a gold mining bonanza. "I remember that little Goldie that worked as a, uh . . . sorta hostess at the Nome Knights Saloon. Now there was a fancy dancer, especially if she had a snoot-full.

"But the sad part was she died. It was that winter when half the town came down with the flu, and it seemed like it was the young ones who died, real fast. They buried her out on the sand-spit—the only place that wasn't frozen solid where you could dig a grave. And then that spring if we didn't have a big high tide, kind like a tidal wave, with the water slushing around right up on Front Street.

"I'll never forget that morning. There was little Goldie, washed up right on the steps of the old Saloon, perfectly preserved, with all that pretty yellow hair spread out so natural, just like she was sleepin' off a drunk. So, then we had to bury her all over again."

On that somber note, even the hard core had gone home and the Victory Ball was history.

Years later, when the tangerine beaded crepe dress was fit only for the rag bag, Mama would look at it and remember the Nome parties and put it back in its box. Eventually she took off the beads and wore it as a nightgown for many more years.

CHAPTER 25

Daddy got a job with the U.S. Engineers that fall, and was working very long hours driving the tractor or the crane they had on the Snake River, getting their projects completed before the heavy snows came. But Mama's job that September was moving from the little shack on Broadway to a house we had found out at the west end of Nome, about ten blocks away. Someone had added a layer of insulation to it not too many years before, and it had an almost new oil burner, and large windows facing the water.

Even though it was a much better house than the old one, Mama wasn't altogether happy about the move. The rent was five dollars more a month, and they still hadn't paid Aunt Lilly for the previous winter's food, much less for the supply which she'd sent on the last boat. We'd paid only a few hundred dollars to the creditors in Seattle since Mama and I had arrived in Nome. So moving into a better house only made her feel guilty, but she felt we couldn't afford to have any of us sick because of the miserable, drafty house we'd been in. It was with misgivings that we decided to move into the high- rent district at twenty-five dollars per month.

By September 19, Mama had worked through the two upstairs bedrooms and the cache leading off the back of the kitchen. That day her plan was to wash down the large kitchen-living room walls, cupboards, windows, and floors, and then start moving in the last of our things. It was very cold that day, with just a powder of fine, dry snow over the frozen ground. When

Mama and I stopped off at Wagner's for some more Lysol on the way to the new house, she bought us each a bright red wool cap that pulled down snug around the face. She knew they would keep our ears warm, and hoped they would perhaps bolster her flagging courage a little.

"How's the housecleaning coming, Alice?" Mabel Wagner asked. "You know, they say once you make the first move, you're really sunk. You'll probably never leave Nome now, girlie. I don't know just what it is about this old hole, but you just get used to it somehow, don't you?"

"Maybe you do, Mabel, but about now I'm kind of discouraged. After moving out of one tumble-down shack into one just like it only bigger, I can take Nome or leave it alone. I said it the first time I walked down Front Street, and I'll say it again: What this town needs is a good fire!"

I could hardly keep my footing against the wild wind that blew us along the street toward the new house. It picked up loose dirt and snow and stung it against our backs as we walked, and finally Mama picked me up, mops, Lysol, and all, and ran the last two blocks to get away from the terribly cold wind. It was still early, about nine, when we arrived, but as soon as Mama got me unbundled, the little girl from next door bustled in to visit. Isabelle was a busy little chatterbox, but Mama said she was glad to see her. She had a couple of her doll children with her, so Mama wouldn't have to have me "helping" her wash walls.

With the two of us playing house over by the warm furnace, the work went quickly, and Mama was surprised when she heard the noon whistle blow. Even though she'd finished washing down the walls and cupboards, and was started on the floor, it seemed she'd only been working an hour or so. Neither of us was hungry, so Mama decided she would finish the floor and put a coat of wax on it before we started back to the old house for lunch. As she worked over toward the windows, she noticed how dark the sky was getting. "You'd better start getting into your outdoor clothes and head for home, Isabelle. It looks like we're going to have a real storm, and your mommy will probably want you home," said Mama.

She was still on her knees on the floor when the door flew open and Daddy banged in, spraying dirty snow all over the still-damp linoleum. "Sure looks nice, Alice, but I'm afraid you washed it all for nothing!"

"Oh no!" she cried. "You mean we can't have the place? After all the cleaning I've done, he certainly can't give it to someone else!"

"No, we can have it, all right. But it's going to burn down! The whole damn town is going to burn down! It started about ten this morning in the old Golden Gate Hotel. That went up like a matchbox, and it's been going like hell ever since. Right through downtown. And as far as I can see, it's not going to stop until there's nothing left to burn . . . . That wind takes the flames a whole block at a time!

"Now listen, Alice, I can't stay with you to help. The two warehouses by the river are already gone and the third one will be next. We've got to get the oil and gasoline out of there first. I've got the cat down there and we're loading the gasoline onto barges and taking it out to sea.

"You better take Artis and go back to the old place and move the rest of the stuff up here. Now listen to me! What you can't take with you . . . just leave it. You won't have time for more than one trip, and keep your eye on the fire, Alice. You can't believe how fast it can move."

"But Jack," Mama asked weakly, "what about the Fire Department? Can't they put it out?"

"Put it out with what, girl? Might as well spit on it as use those two little garden hoses they got. They had, I should say. I don't hear the whistle any more. The fire hall must have burned too, by now."

"But we've got to get those barrels of gas out of there quick, so I'll have to go. I'll meet you here as soon as I can." And he was gone, running off down the wooden plank sidewalk toward the black storm of downtown. Mama noticed that he didn't even have a hat or gloves on, and that his jacket flapped open in the wind.

She said I didn't seem to consider the news of the fire anything too out of the ordinary, but Isabelle, who was seven, was quite concerned. As Mama stuffed her into her parka and mukluks, she gathered her two doll babies into her arms and asked seriously, "Mrs. Palmer, do you suppose we ought to pray?"

Well, Iz," Mama replied, thinking of the whole town's supply of winter food, burned in the two warehouses, "it might be a good idea at that. I'm sure it wouldn't do any harm, anyway."

As soon as she got Isabelle headed for home, Mama bundled me into my parka and red cap and we started back toward town. By this time the huge black clouds of smoke rolled overhead, speckled with cinders and flakes of ashes. Mama said she knew we had to get back to the old house, but all the while her feet wanted to turn and run the other way. The closer she got to town, the faster people were moving, like ants around a disturbed hill. By the time we got back to the Broadway Street house, the activity was frenzied but sporadic. Some people were completely panicked, while others paid no attention to the approaching fire.

When we walked up our front steps, we saw the woman across the street carefully wedging a bushel basket out her second-story window. Finally she got it through the casing and pushed it out, and it splintered open on the wooden sidewalk below, and carefully packed china and crystal flew in all directions. In the living room downstairs, she had her two daughters at work trying to push a large old brass bed out the front door. At the same time we noticed our landlord, who was doing some repairs on the foundation of the old house, going calmly about his work.

Mama hustled me into the house and stationed me at the kitchen window. By this time we could see huge burring brands flying by at terrific speed, about fifty feet in the air. She didn't want to frighten me and tried to control her shaking voice.

"Now listen, baby," she said, "when the church building catches fire, you tell me and we'll get out of here, whether we're all packed or not. Just like a game."

But by then I had found my jacks and ball, and was very bored with the fire game. It simply didn't seem to me like something that was likely to really happen. Fires, except in stoves, were beyond my experience. As Mama threw clothes, pots and pans, shoes, Daddy's tools, and the silverware into a heap on the bed, she left the front door open so she could watch down the street toward the fire. She could feel the wind that screamed by. It was hot and full of tiny cinders that burned small black spots in anything they touched, and Podunk was having a great time trying to chase them. But still the old landlord puttered away at the foundation of the house. Mama jammed our clothes, hangers and all, into the two large suitcases and gathered up the four corners of the bedspread around the bulkier dishes, pans, shoes, and silverware. Fortunately, she had already moved most of our belongings to the new house, but still the chenille knapsack was enormous and very unwieldy.

I said I was hungry and had to have a peanut butter sandwich and some Rice Krispies.

"Sure honey, as soon as we get to the new house, we'll have a nice hot meal," Mama answered, thinking it might be the last one we would have for a long time. She pushed me to the window again, and told me to yell when the church caught fire, while she took one last tour of the house to see that everything was out.

"O.K., baby. We're off. How would you like to carry Daddy's boots?" She tied the laces of the large rubber boots together and hung them over my shoulders, and they barely cleared the ground. Then she put one suitcase under her arm, held the heaviest one by the handle, and slung the bedspread full of housewares over her shoulder, and we bungled down the front steps.

"Say, Mr. Mason, I'm taking your bedspread to carry some of my things in, but we'll get it back to you somehow," Mama yelled at the old man.

"What's the matter, girlie? I thought you wasn't moving till day after tomorrow. I wouldn't worry about the fire if I was you. They'll get it out." He laughed easily.

Jimmy Roach and Cayuse Jack had come out of their cabins too, to watch the fun, and we heard Jimmy cackle to his old partner, "There she goes with her thirty years' collection on her back!"

I was embarrassed at Mama's ungraceful flight and I wished we could forget the whole thing. Besides, Daddy's leather boots were getting very heavy. Down toward town the sky was a solid sheet of flames, but Mama said she knew if she tried to stress the seriousness of the situation to the old men, she would probably cry. So instead she took one last look at the cabin and started away down the street. Cayuse Jack told her several days later, "Ya know, Alice, I never even had time to save my overcoat!"

"Mama look, there goes the Church," I said calmly, as if this were all in a day's work. We watched the steeple blaze up like a slim white candle, and then tried to walk faster, but the one suitcase under Mama's arm kept slipping down and I was floundering badly under the two heavy boots.

As we turned off Broadway onto Front Street, a large burning timber flew onto the flat tar roof of Wagner's store. Almost immediately Mabel Wagner came running out with a step ladder and a tiny fire extinguisher. She dashed up to the roof and pumped madly at the burning roof with her little peashooter, while Mama stood in the street and laughed hysterically until the tears came to her eyes.

Then I remembered something important and started tugging at her arm. "Mama, we forgot my doll clothes that I was washing. They're still in the washing machine, and poor little Shirley won't have anything to change into!" Then Mama remembered that besides all of poor Shirley's clothes, the washer was still full of all our extra sheets, towels, and all the underwear we had, except what we had on. She stopped laughing at Mabel Wagner, but we kept going.

By this time just about everyone in town was in action, and the noise was deafening. The shrieking wind carried burning and crackling boards for two blocks at a fling and threw them against buildings to start new fires. Every dog in town was howling a mournful symphony as they tried to get loose from their chains while Podunk had disappeared completely. Everyone shouted to be heard over the din, but no one took time to listen. They were dynamiting the buildings ahead of the fire to make a firebreak, and the noise and concussion shook the whole town. People ran back and forth across the street loaded with boxes of food, tricycles, suitcases, and bedsteads, usually only to set the things down in the street and head back for more. Little children ran everywhere, some lost and crying, some playing tag and laughing with the excitement.

Just as we passed Wagners' a man started to load his furniture on a pickup truck that had been left standing in the street. There was a new automatic meat saw in the bed of the truck that was in his way, so he just pushed it off the end into the street where the complicated iron parts of the expensive machine shattered as if they were made of crystal. He hoisted on a large overstuffed rocker, two cribs, and an empty bird cage, and drove off toward the edge of town.

I wanted to sit down and rest, so Mama untied the boots and stuffed one into the already bulging bedspread. I carried the other one in my arms and began to cry silently. "I want a drink of water, Mama."

"Stop that whining!" Mama snapped at me. But then my chin began to quiver and I drooped even lower under the heavy load of the boot. So she put down the suitcases and sat me on top of the biggest one.

"Here sweetheart, blow your nose. We'll be there in a few minutes. Just leave the old heavy boot. It doesn't matter." We left the boot standing in the middle of Front Street, and started again. Mama said those boots had cost fifteen dollars, but at that point it seemed completely unimportant whether we saved one of them or two.

As we passed by Precious' house, the Reverend and Mrs. Thorlakkson were just easing the golden oak upright piano out the door and onto the front porch. "Hurry up, fool!" screeched Elva at the straining little man. "Here, let me do it." She gave one mighty heave and the thing skittered off the porch, down the front bank, and onto its teeth in the snow, keys tinkling all the way. They didn't give the ruined piano a second glance. "All right now, Herbert, we've got to save Mother's china cabinet next!" and they fled inside again.

When we got to the new house, Mama set the two suitcases, the bedspread full of junk, and Dad's one boot down inside the porch, thinking she would probably have to move it all again very soon. The fire was headed straight for us and was eating everything in its path. She had just settled me with a bowl of soup, when Daddy and Tagg Samson came in. Tagg was fat and old, and he looked as if he was going to be sick as he slumped down exhausted into a chair, but Daddy was too excited to even sit down. We noticed that his clothes were wet and caked with mud.

"No, I'm not hurt," he insisted impatiently. "I was offshore on the crane loading the last barge of oil when they set off an extra big charge of dynamite, and it knocked me right off the damn thing into the water. That's when I decided it was time to stop loading the barge."

"Why don't you fix some coffee for Tagg and me while I change clothes, Alice. Better make plenty while you're at it. Some of the boys have been fighting this thing for more than three hours now."

But just then Kurt Nordstrom yelled from the porch, "Better get back down there, Jack. We've got another cat from the Army Engineers over across the river, and we're going to blast and level Front Street from Broadway to Kerr!"

Daddy was gone immediately, still in wet clothes, and there was only a cold, black puddle on the floor where he'd been standing. Mama found herself hoping inanely that poor old Mr. Mason had finished the work on the foundation of the house before they blew it up.

Tagg Samson poured himself a cup of coffee and had to steady his elbow on the table as he drank it. "Dammit, Alice, we'll never get that thing put out! You got to have a damn debate with sixteen people before you dynamite one building. Everybody thinks it's going to stop before it gets to their house. But it's not going to stop until there aren't any more houses left to burn. We just can't keep far enough ahead of it to do any good. By the time we get a house cleared out and the charge set, the fire is right there, and when the dynamite blows, it just helps the fire along."

Then Tagg started to laugh weakly. "Alice, you shoulda seen Old Man Sharkey. He's deaf as a board, you know, and I guess maybe he was asleep through the whole thing or something, but anyway, we dynamited Wagner's place right next to his shack. The concussion was enough to knock your teeth out. And out shoots old Sharkey, like a bat out of hell, from that shack of his, with nothing on but his longies. You never saw a more comical look in your life than when the old geezer sees Wagners' store settling around his feet in little pieces, and the damn fire all around him. I tell you, it was rich!"

Tagg was feeling better by the time Daddy and Kurt came back. "I think you better start packing again, Alice. Helga's coming over with her stuff, too. Tagg, we thought maybe you could help the women get the things onto one of the handcars over on the railroad and take it out onto the tundra. It just doesn't look like we've got a chance to stop this thing!"

Daddy and Kurt both looked like old men as they slumped down to drink a cup of coffee. "No, don't bother with sandwiches, Missus," said Kurt. "I don't feel so good for eating." His face was gray with soot, and black sweat outlined his wrinkles. "We just wanted to tell you to start getting out, then we go back to the dynamite."

"Buck Fisher's got the Army fire boat working finally, but I don't think it can do much good against the fire now," said Dad. "It's too big . . . too hot to get close to . . . too fast. And that blasting! Tagg, I tell you, they've gone nuts with it. Every guy in town has got blasting fever. They just take a look in the window, yell to see if anyone answers, and then toss a fistful of lighted sticks in. Kids running around the yards, and women trying to get stuff out right in the middle of it all. If the fire doesn't kill anybody, the damn fools with their dynamite are going to blow someone up for sure!"

"And," Kurt Nordstrom added, "you ought to see them Eskimos. Somebody had the hot idea to get a crew of them together to help take the stuff out of Wagners' store before they blasted it. And by God, if them little devils didn't save the twenty cases of White Horse, first off. They been bellowing around town like a bunch of wild men ever since and Jimmy Roach says he's going to sic 'em onto 'saving' the Whitfield Company's safe full of money next. Says Whitfield owes it to 'em anyway, plus interest."

The men met Helga coming up the walk as they left, and helped her into the house with her impossible load of belongings. She had jammed everything she could into a large steamer trunk, and put it onto Janet's toy red wagon. Then she put the little girl on top, draped Kurt's enormous overcoat over all, and was puffing and tugging it along like a small but sturdy donkey.

"Hello, Alice, I hear we're taking the first coach out of town," said Helga.

Tagg had his pickup truck parked close by and said he would drive us and all we could carry the two miles to the little narrow-gauge railroad at the west end of town that led out onto the tundra. "I'm going to go down to see if I can help Millie Bergdorf, so you girls be ready to go when I get back," he said.

This time Mama's packing was quite different. She didn't bother with the non-essentials like sheets, extra dresses, or silverware and china. Instead, she and Helga emptied the two suitcases and wedged in the wool blankets, a few iron pans, and all the food they could carry—pancake flour, sugar, butter, bread, coffee, and all the canned goods that would fit in.

By the time she had herself and me dressed in every bit of warm clothing we owned, layer upon layer, and Daddy's parka and mukluks over her arm, Tagg had returned with Millie Bergdorf.

"Hi, Helga, Alice. I didn't have much in the way of things to eat to bring along, but I packed plenty of dog food that we can tie into if things get too tough. I didn't know what in hell to do with my dogs, so I let them all loose. I saw Podunk snorting around down by Jack, having a wonderful time. I guess they will all have sense enough to stay out of the fire's way."

They were all ready to go, and Mama said she figured we could live at least a couple of weeks on the food we had with us if there weren't too many to share it with. Tagg loaded both of Helga's suitcases and ours onto the back of the truck, and all five of us squeezed into the cab. We were on our way to the Kougarok Railroad, Ltd. (Very ltd.)

The handcar stood all alone on the narrow tracks as we drove up, so Tagg, Millie, Helga, and Mama hoisted their bundles and trunks and children up onto it. "Now I'll get the thing started for you, and after that, it's a cinch. Just keep the handles pumping up and down and you can't miss." Tagg flicked the mysterious levers and released a crank, and the car started to roll free.

"Here Alice, you're the biggest. You stand behind me, and when I jump off, you grab the handles and pump like hell. Millie, you get on the other end there, and pump that side. Take her out good and far, and then just stop pumping. We'll be out to get you as soon as we can."

Soon Tagg had the car going at a good clickety-clack, Millie took the other end, and he jumped off onto the side of the track. He ran along with us, yelling, "O.K., girls, she's all yours!" Mama stepped into his place, and "pumped like hell," never even taking time to look back to wave at Tagg. First Janet and I started to squeal and giggle, then Helga joined in, and soon all five of us were laughing and howling and snorting and pumping like madwomen. We shrieked over a slight hill and coasted about two miles down the other side at exhilarating speed (probably twenty miles an hour). Finally the car clicked to a stop and we caught our breath and laughed some more.

But as we looked about us and the last chuckle died away, over the vast empty tundra, we were very much alone. It was almost three o'clock, and it was beginning to get dark. Janet and I moved in closer to our mothers, and Helga covered us against the wind with Kurt's overcoat and Dad's extra parka. Then she scrounged around in one of the suitcases and found some homemade sweet rolls, already buttered! We each ate one, and everyone felt a little better and began to look around to see where we'd landed.

"Say, girls," said Millie, pointing out onto the tundra, "I guess we're not so original after all. Look at all the junk out here!" Piled all around us, for about a mile along the tracks, were suitcases and boxes, furniture and food crates, but not another human being in sight. It looked as if half the people in Nome had brought their belongings to this spot. Mama said when they came to get the things later, after the fire was over, lifelong friendships were made and broken as they decided what belonged to whom. But now there was no one to watch the valuables except us, and we couldn't have cared less. Things ceased to have any value whatsoever unless they could be used for food or shelter.

Strangely enough, the fire itself didn't frighten me at all. It was exciting to see the people running around and shouting to each other. But sitting out there on the empty tundra was a different story. I thought of the babes in the woods who were covered over with leaves and never found again. I thought of Hansel and Gretel left to starve in the forest, and I mourned for all of Shirley Temple's clothes still in the washing machine in the old house. And when Mama took her turn to go and look for firewood, I insisted on going along. I'm sure I wasn't much help as a wood-gatherer, but I decided if she was going to get lost, I would at least get lost with her.

When we had scoured the area for about a mile around the handcar, Helga suggested we have a nice cheery campfire. Janet was enchanted with the idea, but I was having none of this cheery nonsense. I was cold and I wanted to go home!

We all looked toward the red, infected-looking smoke clouds over Nome, wondering what there would be left to go home to.

CHAPTER 26

It was almost five-thirty when we saw Daddy and Kurt hiking down the long hill toward us. As they came closer, they looked like two old hobos, clumping very slowly along the side of the narrow railroad tracks, their clothes blackened and ragged.

"Hi, ladies," called Dad, his eyeballs and teeth looking strangely white against his black face. "What's for dinner?"

"Not a thing, unless you can open tin cans with your teeth. We forgot the can opener. Is there anything left at all, Jack?" asked Mama.

"Yeah, we finally stopped it. The U.S. Engineers got the fire boat working and maneuvered it up the river. Every guy in town helped with the dynamiting, and then Kurt and I each took a cat and leveled about four square blocks. We took the big tarps and a bunch of old tents the Army gave us, and covered up the whole four blocks with them. Then the fire boat sprayed the tarps down with river water, and that finally stopped it. I don't think we would have had a chance even then, if the wind hadn't stopped just at the right time."

"Yeah, as soon as we spray one spot and go on to the next, then the first one is sizzling already," added Kurt. "Them tarps on the end by the fire sure isn't much good for anything again. They're all scorched through in big holes . . . not just on the one end either. The flames licked out as far as forty feet over the wet canvas!"

"I know what you mean, Kurt. I didn't say it at the time, but when we'd been spraying for about a half hour steady, I sure thought we should have saved our breath. And saved the tarps, too. I knew they were going to bum, and I was thinking how bad we'd need the canvas to make tents out of. When all of a sudden, it was like the fire had enough of teasing us. The wind got tired of the game, and that was all there was to it."

"But what a mess we got there! It's getting colder already. You know how it gets when the wind turns off. It will be probably below freezing tonight and there's only a few blocks of houses left. And some of them Eskimos is drunker than ever!"

"Oh, by the way, Alice," added Daddy, "I forgot to tell you. Our house is all right. We didn't have time to figure too much out, but the men decided that each house left will have to take in about ten extra people. I saw Tagg Samson and already told him he could stay with us. He found Joe Easiola and the boy and of course you, Millie, and Helga and Kurt and Janet will be staying at our place too. Palmer's Flop House, now open for business!"

Kurt and Daddy soon had the handcar rolling, and in a few minutes we were flying home. And "home" was a wonderful thought at that point. All that late afternoon, Millie and Helga and Mama had taken turns scouting the tundra around the handcar for wood to burn that night, and now we were actually going home! Mama said that just to have Daddy and me both safe and with her, and to have a house to sleep in that night seemed almost too much good fortune for one woman. She remembered, as we clicked over the narrow rails toward Nome, my little friend Isabelle saying, "Do you suppose we ought to pray, Mrs. Palmer?" and right then seemed like a perfect time to do just that.

But as we approached Nome, it looked as if a war had just finished where our town used to be. Several areas were still smoking, but most of the town was black and still and dead. We couldn't even identify the streets, because the wooden sidewalks had burned and the rubble of the buildings had been crushed over into the roads by the tractors. We could look right out over where the heart of the town used to be. It had burned straight down to the water line, and only the cold Bering Sea stretched beyond.

"Look, Alice," said Dad, pointing to what must have been Front Street, "those two concrete blocks sticking up are the vaults from Welty's bank. The only things in town that didn't burn, but they're so badly melted it looks like they'll have to be blasted open."

The canvas was still down over the blasted area, and beyond that firebreak stood the few houses left. It was already quite dark and every house left standing was lit up and bursting with company. By the sounds of celebration coming from almost every house, we figured some Eskimos weren't the only ones who had helped to "save" the town's bottled goods.

Helga and Millie and Mama unpacked the food suitcases in our kitchen and served dinner in three shifts, first to Janet and Maxwell and me and also to the old man. Then Daddy, Kurt, and Tagg Samson ate, and finally the women sat down to biscuits, luncheon meat, and canned beans. The three men ate like a team of threshers, but Joe Easiola was so confused and upset by the fire, it was pitiful to watch him.

"Seems like the whole town went crazy this afternoon, Miz Palmer," he complained feebly to Mama. "Everybody runnin' round and hollerin' and yellin'. And they say there was a fire in the hotel! But the Golden Gate is O.K., ain't it?"

"Sure Joe, everything is fine, but we want you and Maxwell to stay here tonight anyway. Just rest easy and everything will be fine in the morning," said Mama.

As soon as they got the three of us children to sleep in my bed, they made beds out of the couch and chair cushions on the floor in the living room for the men. Helga and Millie and Mama took the double bed upstairs, but after the house was dark and quiet, and Kurt and Joe Easiola were snoring softly, Mama found she was too tired to sleep. She threw Dad's coat over her shoulders and made her way carefully around the sleeping men into the kitchen. She lit only one lamp in the far corner of the room, but found that Daddy was still awake too, so she put the coffee pot back on the stove to warm. The cups were still packed somewhere, so she poured out a couple of water glasses full of coffee.

While they waited for it to cool, they could hear the sound of people laughing and squealing and singing all over the town, through the cold still air. "Tagg was saying they checked all over, and there wasn't one person even hurt. Anna and Joseph and all their gang are O.K. although some of them are going to have the granddaddy of all hangovers tomorrow. Jimmy Roach has taken his wife and kids over to stay with the savages across the river, as he calls them. The Blue Fox is open for business as usual under one of those damn tarps that didn't get burned . . . nothing but White Horse to drink, they say! Nobody even got blown up! Seems hard to believe, doesn't it?" asked Daddy.

"Just like a miracle! Especially with all that blasting. And he said they saved the third food warehouse too, which is . . . . .Say Jack, have you tasted this coffee? It must be what was left from the stuff I fixed you during the fire before we left. Good Lord, I must have added coffee to it at least six times! It's so strong, you practically have to chew it!" Mama started laughing, but all of a sudden she was crying instead.

"Now, Alice Palmer," protested Daddy, "after all we've been through today, you're not going to let a bum pot of coffee get you down!"

"Oh no, it's not the coffee, Jack. I just want to go home, that's all! This is like a nightmare, being trapped in this God forsaken hole! What are we doing here, anyway? No money, no job, now no town even," she sobbed. "Jack, what are we going to *do*?"

"What are we going to do! Why, we're going to rebuild Nome, of course! What are you thinking of, girl? We're sitting in the golden chair. I'm the only guy in town with a box of tools and the know-how to use them. I tell you, we're sitting in the golden chair, at last! Now dry your eyes, and get some sleep. I have a feeling tomorrow's going to be a busy day."

CHAPTER 27

A s it turned out, Daddy was right. We were, at last, in the right place at the right time, and from that day on our lives were turned toward prosperity again.

The Red Cross representative arrived on a specially chartered plane into Nome the day after the fire. He and Dad met with the agent from the Alaska Steamship Company all the rest of that afternoon. As they sat at the kitchen table trying to make a detailed list of all the building materials needed to reconstruct a town, practically every man with a burned-out home or business stopped in to get Dad started immediately on rebuilding their house or store or bank or restaurant.

"Listen, Palmer," Mr. Wagner demanded, "Wagner Commercial *is* Nome! The Red Cross can haul all the stuff in here they want but they've got to have a store building big enough to keep it in and distribute it from. My store and the two warehouses have got to be first!"

"Simmer down, damn it, Joe," interrupted Jake Welty. "I know all the merchants figure their places are pretty important, but after all, first things first. Nobody in town will be able to make a move until we can get the bank going again, and I can't work out of our living room for the rest of the winter. I've got to have my bank rebuilt before the snow comes, and I've got the cash to pay for it right here, Jack. Like I said, nobody makes a move without the bank!"

"The hell they don't!" shouted Ed Stern, the young man who ran the Blue Fox Saloon. "Ethel's having that baby next month whether your bank keeps or rots, and we've got to have a place to live . . . I know you won't have time for a firm bid, Jack. You just go ahead on the thing and we'll settle up as you go along. Cost plus fifteen per cent sound O.K.? Maybe Alice could write us up an agreement and I could sign it right now."

And so it went, all that day and most of the night. Until finally Dad and the men from the Red Cross and Alaska Steamship had to escape upstairs to work in the bedroom, while Mama tried to reassure everyone in Nome that he would positively have their work done by the time the snow came.

Elva Thorlakkson had the blame for the fire neatly pinpointed to the sinners in town. "I always did say this town was a hotbed of sin. Carousing and drinking and all those natives and all! God's wrath is a terrible thing!" she insisted happily.

But if Elva was right, God had had enough of His wrath, because that year Nome had the mildest winter on record at the weather station since before 1900. The town held its breath while the two special emergency supply ships made their way toward Nome from Seattle, sneaking through waters that were usually solid ice by that time of year. It was the last week in September when the two ships anchored off Nome, and it had always been the unwritten law that no vessel ever sailed the Bering Sea north of the Aleutian Islands after October first.

They loaded the clumsy barges with the food and other emergency supplies to be lightered into Nome with desperate speed. The crew didn't even take time to put the lumber onto the barges, but merely dumped it into the water to float into Nome on the incoming tide. None of the men were allowed time to come ashore, and by the time Kurt Nordstrom had hauled the first load of lumber up off the beach with the tractor, both ships were gone and out of sight.

It was a good thing that Daddy was in good shape from the past lean years, or he never could have kept up the pace of the following months. Every morning we were up by six o'clock, and he was out on the jobs by seven, several hours before daylight, to lay out the day's work with the lead man on each job. Mama usually packed a lunch for him so he could spend the hour at noon discussing the various plans with the owners or sub-contractors or suppliers. By four in the afternoon it was too dark and too cold to work on anything except the few buildings which were already closed in, so he was usually home by five. Then as soon as we finished dinner, Mama would put on another pot of coffee and Dad would draw plans, often until two or three the next morning, trying to keep a day or so ahead of the workmen on each job.

Our "carpenters" were fishermen and gold-miners, cannery-workers and pursers off the boats, but they all learned fast with the wind off the Bering Sea at their backs. Tagg Samson worked as labor foreman that winter with twenty to thirty Eskimos as his crew. Tagg's only association with the Eskimos before then was when some of them got drunk and he had to haul them into his jail to sober up, so naturally he didn't have too high an opinion of his men. Tagg himself, even though he was old and had a huge beer-belly, was strong as an ox, and couldn't stand to see the natives struggling for hours on a job that he felt he could have done himself in minutes.

On one of the rare sunny afternoons in October, Mama and I went down to watch the progress on the new Post Office job. Dad was laying out the work for the next morning with Tagg, while three of the Eskimos wrestled with a boulder that was in the way of the foundation for the porch. It wasn't a very big rock, but it was round and smooth and almost impossible for the men to get a hold of. We could tell that Tagg was embarrassed to have Dad see his men doing so poorly at the task. The big man watched as long as he could stand it, his face getting redder by the minute, and then he turned to the three natives and their rock. "Get outa here, ya little ninnies. Let me do it!"

But Tagg was too fast. One small worker was left clinging to the boulder, eyes open wide and feet dangling in the air, as Tagg lifted the rock, clumps of tundra and dirt, Eskimo and all, shoulder high and plunked it down out of the way.

But what the Eskimos lacked in strength and skill, they made up for with hard work and enthusiasm. Before we were through, Daddy was convinced that even Tagg Samson was beginning to like and understand them better. One evening, as he and Tagg talked over the following day's plans, we heard Daddy trying to explain his views about the natives to the older man.

"You've really done a swell job with that gang of yours, Tagg. They've put out more work than you even expected yourself, haven't they? And you know, I've said, right from the first time I had anything to do with the Eskimos, if you treat them with respect, and explain things carefully, and try halfway to get along, they're O.K. It pays off."

"Why sure, boy. I know exactly what you mean. I've dealt with those natives for years here in Nome, and I've said the same thing. You just got to get their confidence, before you really put the spurs into 'em, that's all."

But, all in all, The Palmer Construction Company had surprisingly little trouble in rebuilding the little town. Of course, there was the usual red tape with credit for the people trying to build, especially after Jake Welty went into the contracting business. Daddy's customers found it almost impossible to borrow money from the bank until the cache and the whole front end of the living room fell off of Welty Construction's first house. Soon after that, Jake went back into the money-changing game and things went smoother.

Then Elva Thorlakkson found out somehow that Daddy had been brought up as a Catholic, and insisted on coming down twice a day for a personal inspection of the new church building. She and Precious would teeter over the planks and timbers in their slippery galoshes (they never sank to wearing the sensible Eskimo mukluks), watching suspiciously to see if any secret agents of the Pope had infiltrated the place. She just about drove the men wild, looking down their necks while they worked, but soon it was too cold even for Elva.

The foundation on the new Federal Post Office was just about finished when the additions and changes to the plans started pouring in, Special Delivery, Air Mail, hot off the drawing board of some Civil Service architect down in Arizona. There it was; all low, flat-top roof and huge, airy plate-glass windows. It would have been perfect for Arizona, or even California in a long, hot, dry spell, but not Nome! Daddy rushed several lengthy, expensive telegrams back to Arizona explaining why this plan would never work in Nome—how the seventy-mile-an-hour winds would crush in the large glass areas like eggshells, what would happen to the large flat-top roof when it had to support several tons of wet snow.

But the only answer he ever received arrived a month later saying tersely:

```
CONTRACTOR TO ADHERE TO PLANS EXPLICITLY  STOP
REPEAT EXPLICITLY  STOP  ADDENDUM #4, CHANGES
#712 TO 978 TO FOLLOW  STOP
```

As it happened, we found out much later that Addendum #4, including changes 712 to 978, was sent by mistake to confuse some other poor contractor working on a Federal Court House in the Territory of Hawaii, instead of the Territory of Alaska.

But anyway, by this time Dad had gone ahead on his own and filled in more than half the glass area with sturdy brick, and put on a good steep-pitched roof. He said he figured he owed the Government about ten years in Federal Prison for the bootlegging they had done anyway, and he could serve both sentences at the same time.

The official sent up from Fairbanks to give the job the final inspection was a retired superintendent of schools. His top-coat wasn't nearly heavy enough, the food at the hotel was not agreeing with him, and he was anxious to be home for Thanksgiving. Daddy helped him hold his brand new tape while he measured the building to see that it was the specified size; he took a quick tour of the inside, carefully checking faucets and light switches to see that they were in good order, and he was finished.

"It really looks lovely to me, Mr. Palmer. I'm sure you've done a fine job," he shivered. "Personally, I can't see how they can get qualified men to work in such a place!" He left on the next plane for Fairbanks, and the architect in Arizona was never the wiser.

The bitter wind blew constantly on and on, in from the sea, but by the end of November Daddy had about twenty houses, the Post Office, the bank, both warehouses, and Wagners' store, the church, and the two taverns almost completely closed in. He borrowed about fifty small stoves from the Army Engineers and kept several of them burning in each building night and day. They didn't provide any real comfort, but at least they took the worst of the chill out of the half-finished rooms and kept the nails from freezing to the men's hands as they had done constantly when they'd been working outside. Daddy said he would reach into the nail keg to pick out a few nails, and his hand would come out covered with them, bristling out like porcupine quills.

Every day the old men would predict the break in the weather. "That light greenish cast in the sky in the afternoon is a dead giveaway, boys. Yep, I figure we'll see the end of the good weather come the end of the week. Monday by the latest."

So the men worked a little faster and Dad stayed up with the plans a little later every night. By Christmas, several families had moved in, planning to do their own finishing work. Gradually the final payments on the work started to come in, and it began to look as if the Palmers would be in the big time once more. None of the homes had been lavishly done, but each one brought in a little profit, and the theater and the two taverns each paid very well on the cost-plus basis.

Still, Christmas was simple that year. Everyone was working too hard to take time off, still racing against the snow they knew must come soon. And of course, there was very little in the town to buy for presents. But just the same, the Christmas of that winter was one of the highlights of our life. Late in the afternoon of Christmas Eve we all hiked down to the emergency radio station set up at the Army base, and cabled the balance of all the money we owed. To Ernst Hardware, Elliott Bay Lumber, Pioneer Sand and Gravel, Fuller Paints, Acme Painting and Decorating, and to Star Electric.

Mama and Daddy were both too tired to celebrate or to even talk much about having paid the ancient debts at last.

But we walked home through the sparkling cold afternoon real fast. And, as Mama said, "I've never felt younger, before or since. Months and years later, I still find myself dividing up imaginary paychecks in my dreams. Thirty per cent to Ernst, fifteen per cent for the painter, forty per cent to Elliott—only to wake up in a cold sweat, and tell myself it's all paid, all over at last."

But finally, a day after New Year's, the snow did come. It came in a roar of white, blanketing, paralyzing cold. But by that time, we were ready for it. All the buildings were battened down for the winter, and the little stoves sputtered cozily while the carpenters and painters did their finishing.

CHAPTER 28

There were a lot of changes in Nome that winter. The old town was gone, and even the old men had to move into new houses. Millie Bergdorf took old Joe Easiola and her "son" Maxwell in with her. But from the time the Golden Gate burned, the old man grew more vague and confused. It was only six months after the fire that Joe Easiola died easily in his sleep. Millie rebuilt her tavern, but shortly after Joe's funeral, she sold out and opened a nice, family-style restaurant instead.

Kurt Nordstrom saved almost everything he earned working for Daddy that winter, and in March he and Helga bought out the Snake River Exploratory Corporation. Edgar St. George went home to England that spring, and the last we heard of Count Barkavitch, he was heading for Florida to be a real-estate magnate.

And Gust and Florence had a baby that spring. Although Elva Thorlakkson said it was a shame, a middle-aged woman carrying on like that, Gust confided to Mama, after pressing several large cigars on Daddy, "You know, Missus, I thought I would never get over missing my old dog, Shorty, and them pups of hers that I never got to see even. But after waiting with Florence in the hospital, so big and calm, and then seeing that little one, already with fingernails and eyelashes and all! Well, I tell you, I've been a fool all along up to now. Oh, Shorty was a good enough dog, all right, but to have a good woman and children to love. That's really what it's all about, ain't it?"

Then he blushed again, stuffed a couple more cigars into Daddy's hand, and barged out.

By early spring it was just as Daddy had said. The Palmers were sitting pretty, with money in the bank and more work coming up as soon as the spring thaw. But it seems there always comes a time to go home. It was April when the time came for us. Nome was well again, rebuilt better and stronger than ever before, and so were we. The little town had given us friends and memories to last a lifetime. We'd landed there in desperation, with no more than the clothes we wore and borrowed food for the first winter, without even our pride intact. We left with the debts paid and a feeling that we'd done a good job.

That spring Uncle Max wrote that Seattle seemed to be reviving at last. Max added that he couldn't stand much more of "this damn civilian life, sitting around on my haunches, just battin' the breeze, year after year!" Besides that, he said it rained too much in Seattle, and he wanted to go back in the Navy.

"Things begin to look kind of phony in Europe, and they could probably use an old Chief or two to tell the punk Lieutenants what to do. Kind of hate to leave Ma alone, though. Write soon what your plans are."

By this time I was "going on six," and had reached the long, thin stage where I looked like a good candidate for rickets, and Mama felt perhaps some rich, fresh milk and fruit and vegetables, and a warmer climate, might do me some good.

Anyway, it was time to go home, and the more we thought about it, the better it seemed. Suddenly we were hungry for the sight of green grass with a few daffodils poking through, and blossoms on the fruit trees, and the sound of frogs talking down in back of the ranch. Mama tried to remember the feeling of sunshine, lying on the beach at Alki, too hot to reach over for the lemonade. But it was impossible . . . too long ago. We could almost taste the first thin asparagus, young cucumbers still cool from Grama's garden, and the tiny wild blackberries floating in thick, purpled cream.

About that time, Aunt Lilly wrote that she and Uncle August felt it was time for their son to take over the grocery store, and they wanted a house built on the Lake, where they could moor their boat. She wondered if Daddy would consider drawing the plans and building a home for them.

That did the trick! The first boat couldn't come soon enough for us, so Fritz Niemyer, one of the bush pilots, said we could fly down to Seattle with him if we didn't mind a few mail sacks along on the trip. Daddy finished the last clean-up work on the last job by the middle of the month, and a couple of days later, almost as quickly as we'd prepared for the trip coming to Nome two years before, we were packed and ready to leave.

The afternoon of the day before we were to leave, the Ladies' Aid gave a farewell tea at the new church. Mrs. Rosetti made several wooden freezers full of Spumoni, and Tessie Welty brought the sheet cake with pink roses and "Bon Voyage, Alice" on the top. The ladies drank coffee and exchanged addresses and Mama promised to call on all the sisters and friends and mothers in Seattle. Helga came in from Cripple Creek to say good-by and pick up Podunk for adoption.

"What on earth will happen to the social set of Nome without us, Helga," whispered Mama. "With you at Cripple Creek all summer and me leaving, Elva Thorlakkson will probably have everyone back on the straight-and-narrow again!"

Along with all the other Nome ladies, Elva was there too. In fact she insisted on giving Mama a soft, damp kiss and a speech on "leaving dear friends behind, never to be seen again in this world!"

"Ah hell, Elva, what are you talking about?" groused Mabel Wagner. "Alice and Jack are sourdoughs now. You know you can never really stay outside once you've seen the ice break, girl!"

But Mama knew she wouldn't see Nome again.

The morning that we were supposed to leave it started to snow. Sometimes it was heavy, thick feathers piling up four to six feet a day. Others it was spiteful little drifts, blowing from one side of the yard to the other. But for three weeks, nothing moved in or out of Nome.

Each day we wakened early, eager for the sight of blue sky, or even a high cloud ceiling. And each morning it was the same—dense, low-hanging clouds and fitful snow flurries. The temperature stayed the same also; about ten degrees below zero during the day, and then it would drop down to twenty or thirty below as soon as darkness fell late in the afternoon.

All the parties had been given, all the hands shaken, all the farewell toasts drunk. Jimmy Roach had copied and recopied his latest letter for Mama to give to the governor of Washington as soon as she happened to see him. All our clothes, except for what we would wear to travel in, were packed. And so we sat waiting in great style, but very little comfort, for the weather to lift.

Mama had taken down the curtains and pictures. The books and tablecloths and towels and carpets and all the other small human things that make life livable were either stuffed into the foot-lockers or pawned off on the neighbors. Our stripped house looked as impersonal and unfriendly as though we had never lived there. When Mama stopped the brass pendulum on the clock and wrapped it in a pair of flannel pajamas on top of the last suitcases, the silence was deafening. All the sad songs had been sung, the serpentine thrown, the whistle blown; and yet we had to stay on. "Snowbound" was no longer merely a quaint, old-fashioned term.

We wouldn't even have known when it was time to eat lunch, except for the dogs all over town howling in unison at twelve sharp every day. The noon whistle had never been replaced after the fire, but the Huskies still remembered. You could set your watch by the dogs' serenade every day at twelve noon exactly.

Meals were pretty sketchy affairs anyway, as we were trying to use up all the canned food from the past winter instead of buying too much ahead. Every morning we would all hike down to the weather station to hear what the Coast Guard had to say about the possibility of flying. With a great many technical terms and fancy diagrams they would say, "Maybe so . . . maybe not. Wait and see." Then on the way home, we'd stop by the store and pick up the meat for dinner and whatever else of interest Mabel Wagner had to offer. Sometimes it was canned green beans on special, sometimes the newest development on Tessie Welty's gallstones.

"Say, Alice," she said one day, "I hear you folks are flying down with Fritz Niemyer. He was in this morning for another case of club soda, and looking dignified as all getout. I guess you know what that means!"

ALMOST EVERYONE WHO LIVED IN Nome all year round was a little peculiar in one way or another, but the bush pilots of northern Alaska were in a class by themselves. Not only did they have to be pilot, navigator, and expert mechanics on their spindly little airplanes; but they also needed to know a good deal of midwifery, how to live for three weeks at a time on seal blubber and dried tom-cod, and what to do for alcohol poisoning. Most of them were the dregs and/or the cream of the crop of World War I pilots, half poltergeist, half hero. And Fritz Niemyer was no exception.

He had lost his commercial pilot's license the summer before for buzzing so close to an Eskimo village that the chief's favorite daughter, who was pregnant at the time, had panicked and fallen and killed herself. That winter after the fire, though, pilots were too badly needed to inquire into their credentials. So Fritz was working steady again, between benders.

You could always tell when the big red-headed German was drunk. After enough Scotch and soda to kill an average earth-bound man, Fritz merely became stately. He would walk very straight lines, turn square corners, and hold his head as though he were wearing a monocle in each eye. He would hold forth at one end of the Blue Fox bar, speaking slowly and distinctly of profound subjects. He would tell how Alsace-Lorraine should have been handled, or explain the outer galaxies. Then folks knew that Fritz wouldn't last too much longer. So when Mabel Wagner reported that he had been seen looking dignified, we knew that not too many hours would pass before Fritz would fall like a pole-axed bronze, and it would take four strong men to carry him to his bed.

"Well, I guess we can stop worrying about the weather, anyway," snorted Mama. "By the time Fritz sobers up we can pile the foot-lockers in a canoe and paddle down to Seattle ourselves!"

With the perversity of Nome weather, the next morning dawned clear and cold. It was the first time the sun had shown itself in three weeks and could very well be the last for another three. As soon as we opened our eyes, Mama gasped, "Jack, you better check on Fritz Niemyer right after breakfast. Pour water on him or something. Tell him the mail must go through!"

By ten, the dishes were done and packed, we were dressed in our best "white" clothes, and Kurt and Helga had arrived with the little yellow tractor for the trip out to the airstrip. Everything and everyone was ready—everyone but Fritz Niemyer. Poor Fritz lay where he'd fallen the night before, spread-eagled on one of the tables in the Blue Fox Saloon, like a stunned ox.

By eleven, all of Nome was working on the problem, but our pilot neither spoke nor batted an eye. Miss Eckmann up at the hospital suggested a fourth of a cupful of straight honey, insisting that a hangover is nothing but a simple lack of sugar in the blood. But no one know how to get the honey down his gullet.

"Give him a bit of the hair o' the dog," crooned Jimmy Roach. "I wasn't a saloonkeeper all those years for nothin', ya know," he said, tenderly cradling Fritz's unconscious head in his arms, and pouring down a generous cupful of lukewarm beer mixed with a raw egg and Tabasco sauce. The only result of the "prairie oyster" was a bad case of hiccups.

Big Nick and Gust even helped Daddy carry the helpless, hopeless form all the way down to the new Finnish Baths. They steamed him for an hour, with one of Einar's massage treatments thrown in for free. Still Fritz couldn't or wouldn't open his eyes.

There were a lot of experts in Nome on the care and treatment of hangovers, and they tried every cure known to man, and some originals never heard of before or since. Still . . . nothing.

By two that afternoon Mama was literally wringing her hands. The U.S. Marshal had arrived with seven huge sacks of mail for "outside" that had been piling up during the bad weather. He was muttering about "taking proper legal steps" and jail and hangings and lynching parties, but Fritz snoozed on.

Finally, it was Millie Bergdorf who saved the day again. She left her lunch customers to fend for themselves as best they could, and headed for the Finnish Baths.

"Leave me have a try at that fool Kraut. He always bragged about flying those one-lungers in 1916, but nobody ever mentioned whose side he was on. I got one of my bright ideas comin' on!"

With that, she muscled her way into Einar's bathhouse where the body reposed, swung through the doors that no woman had ever swung before, and took a deep breath. Then, in the voice that once electrified the last row of the Tivoli Burlesque Palace, she bellowed directly into Fritz's sleeping face.

"Achtung, du Lousepoop! Hoch der Kaiser! Deutchland über Alles!"

Fritz arose to his full height, clicked his heels together, and marched glassy-eyed out the door toward Broadway and the waiting tractor-in his undershirt. Jimmy Roach threw a mangy-looking parka over his head and shoulders, and it began to look as though we might make Fairbanks after all.

The pilot was very hazy about what had happened at the Finnish Baths to bring him back to life, but he wasn't happy about it. He felt he had betrayed himself somewhere along the line, and wouldn't speak a word as Kurt drove us out onto the tundra. Instead he clapped his goggles and helmet over his head and snorted through his shaggy red mustache.

With the snow from the past weeks, the town looked new—washed and neat, with its white toy houses and stores and streets, and the black burned part covered with snow. The tundra was drifted over, smooth and hard, a perfect runway for Fritz's spindly-looking plane. It was at least twenty degrees below zero when we reached the strip, but there was a good-sized crowd gathered to see us off. There was no hangar for the little plane, of course, but there was a small three-sided dog house thrown together of ship-lap and canvas, called a nose hangar, used to keep the engine from freezing.

As Mamma and I huddled together with Helga and Janet in the tiny warming hut, Daddy and Fritz hopped down off the cat and shoved the small tent arrangement away to start heating the nose and its innards.

The old Eskimo chief poked his head into the warming hut and motioned to Mama. "You tell Jack Palmer my Anna says the snow will come soon again. One, two hours. Maybe you stay Nome little more?"

"Oh no, Joseph. We have to go now. The rent was up on the house two weeks ago and the new tenants are waiting to move in. Today's the day. We just have to get off today!"

"Now Alice, don't get nervous," said Helga soothingly. "Fritz looks like his old self again, and see, Kurt is draining the oil out of the plane already. They have the blowtorch going in the nose hangar to heat up the engine, and we can heat the oil on the stove in here. You'll be taking off in less than a half hour now."

While Kurt heated the oil drained from the engine in a four-pound coffee can on top of the oil burner, Fritz pulled a half-full bottle of whisky out of the desk drawer.

"Chust about ready, Missus. A little drink we have for the cold, a nice dose of warm oil for 'Liebchen', and we go."

The hut was full of oil and whisky fumes, so we moved outside. The wind was blowing again off the sea, and cut through our heavy woolen clothes as if they were tissue paper. A couple of the young Eskimo men were heaving in the mail sacks, along with various bulky boxes of groceries, and a very large frozen reindeer carcass. Anna shaded her eyes with her hand as she looked out at the sky above the ice ocean.

"Time to hurry, Ah-leece! Snow comes soon!"

Then the small, wrinkled woman called to her husband and the group of Eskimos with him. Anna had a pair of soft fur-slippers for Mama and me, and when she handed me my pair, she gave me a kiss, Eskimo style, rubbing her little stubby nose against mine. Then she reached up and took Mama's face in her small hands.

"Ah-leece, I feel you and me just like cousins. Too much sad I don't see you and Baby and Jack Palmer again!"

Then old Joseph stepped forward and presented Dad with a pair of intricately beaded wolf-head mitts. The eye and nose slits were filled in with tiny, light blue beads, and the whiskers and ruff around the face carefully left on, so that when he put them on his hands and held the palms together, they made a wolf's head.

"Jack Palmer, we give a little thing, but our hearts is very big," said Joseph Aloruk. "For all the beach wood you haul in the yellow engine for our fires. For the good work you give the men. For helping to build better houses for us. The men in the village say Jack Palmer is good hunter . . . very big man!"

Daddy put the beautiful beaded gloves on and shook the old man's hand to thank him, when suddenly the young men who were loading the plane started to shout.

Bright orange flames were licking out from the rickety board and canvas hangar, directly under Liebchen's engine. Fritz streaked out of the hut with a tiny fire extinguisher, while everyone dug madly at the packed runway, trying to throw snow onto the fire. Fritz aimed the little stream of chemical at the flames, while Daddy shoved the portable hangar away from the plane.

When the smoke and excitement died down, it turned out that only the canvas flaps on the hangar were burned. The blow-torch used to heat the engine had exploded and was a total loss. Our teeth were chattering like castanets, but Liebchen was as good as ever.

Fritz poured the warm oil in, as Daddy hoisted Mama and me into the crowded cabin. We wedged our trembling bodies in among the ice-cold mail sacks, and Daddy slammed the cabin door shut. He shared his seat with the stiff reindeer carcass, and I sat on Mama's lap so I could see out the window.

Then Fritz motioned for the crowd to stand back, and we taxied around in a large arc. Soon the plane picked up speed, faster and faster, and suddenly we were free. We were flying. Fritz circled around once to dip the wings at the small people on the snow, and then we passed over Nome, still asleep like a dark smudge on the white tundra.

Mama held me higher for one last look at the town, and said in a slightly shaking voice, "Well Jack, now that we're actually going, I don't know whether I'm glad or sad. One thing's for sure, though. There's no place like Nome!"

Then we headed south and east, toward home.

CPSIA information can be obtained at www.ICGtesting.com
Printed in the USA
BVOW02s1417290713

326920BV00002B/2/P